The Guru of Golf

ALSO BY THOMAS MOORE

The Planets Within

Rituals of the Imagination

A Blue Fire

Dark Eros

Care of the Soul

Meditations

Soul Mates

The Re-Enchantment of Everyday Life

The Education of the Heart

The Book of Job

The Soul of Sex

Original Self

The Soul's Religion

Dark Nights of the Soul

A Life at Work

*Writing in the Sand**

*Care of the Soul in Medicine**

*Available from Hay House

Please visit:

Hay House USA: **www.hayhouse.com®**
Hay House Australia: **www.hayhouse.com.au**
Hay House UK: **www.hayhouse.co.uk**
Hay House South Africa: **www.hayhouse.co.za**
Hay House India: **www.hayhouse.co.in**

The Guru of Golf

And Other Stories about the Game of Life

Thomas Moore

HAY HOUSE, INC.
Carlsbad, California • New York City
London • Sydney • Johannesburg
Vancouver • Hong Kong • New Delhi

Copyright © 2010 by Thomas Moore

Published and distributed in the United States by: Hay House, Inc.: www.hayhouse.com • ***Published and distributed in Australia by:*** Hay House Australia Pty. Ltd.: www.hayhouse.com.au • ***Published and distributed in the United Kingdom by:*** Hay House UK, Ltd.: www.hayhouse.co.uk • ***Published and distributed in the Republic of South Africa by:*** Hay House SA (Pty), Ltd.: www.hayhouse.co.za • ***Distributed in Canada by:*** Raincoast: www.raincoast.com • ***Published in India by:*** Hay House Publishers India: www.hayhouse.co.in

Design: Julie Davison

All rights reserved. No part of this book may be reproduced by any mechanical, photographic, or electronic process, or in the form of a phonographic recording; nor may it be stored in a retrieval system, transmitted, or otherwise be copied for public or private use—other than for "fair use" as brief quotations embodied in articles and reviews—without prior written permission of the publisher.

The author of this book does not dispense medical advice or prescribe the use of any technique as a form of treatment for physical, emotional, or medical problems without the advice of a physician, either directly or indirectly. The intent of the author is only to offer information of a general nature to help you in your quest for emotional and spiritual well-being. In the event you use any of the information in this book for yourself, which is your constitutional right, the author and the publisher assume no responsibility for your actions.

Library of Congress Cataloging-in-Publication Data

Moore, Thomas.
The guru of golf : and other stories about the game of life / Thomas Moore.
p. cm.
ISBN 978-1-4019-2565-9 (hardcover : alk. paper)
1. Golf--Philosophy. I. Title.
GV967M715 2010
796.352--dc22

2010000393

Tradepaper ISBN: 978-1-4019-2566-6

14 13 12 11 5 4 3 2
1st edition, June 2010
2nd edition, September 2011

Printed in the United States of America

To my father, Ben Moore,
who taught me the game.

CONTENTS

PREFACE

In my first year of playing golf, I was hitting balls consistently in the woods that lined the fairways in the New Hampshire courses near my home. One day I was with three good players and hit a long ball from the tee that came within inches of the hole. One of my teammates put his head on the green to measure how close the ball was to going in. I have never come that close again. That day I learned about the capriciousness and magic of the game.

My graduate school professor of religion, David L. Miller, who wrote the wonderful book *Gods and Games*, taught me much about the connection between games and rituals. He says that games are much more profound than we imagine. It wasn't difficult for me to go from playing golf to writing stories that border the regions of sport and the sacred.

Early on I told a few friends about these golf stories, and they assumed I would be writing teaching stories under the guise of golf. That is not my intention. I don't write stories aimed at offering moral or spiritual lessons. I like stories as stories. If they hold up on their own, I'm happy. I think games do teach us about life and beyond, and I hope these stories offer hints at some of the mysteries involved in the game of life. But most of all, I hope the stories are entertaining. All art, I assume, helps us appreciate the deep mysteries we confront every day, and in that sense all art is theological.

These stories came to me one day when I had much more pressing things to do. But they were so strong and so consistent in their arrival that I had to write them. I think an author should never know fully what his or her story is about. I respected the characters and plots and scenes that appeared to me. I wished that some of them might be more explicitly "spiritual" and that a few might end differently. But they are as they came to me.

Maybe because I have written a number of "heavy" books, when I write fiction, the humor comes out strong. But I think good spiritual writing ought to be funny. Laughter breaks us free of our too serious secularism.

I started playing golf in earnest late in life, after a diagnosis of heart disease. I'm not a golf fanatic, and I'm not good at the game. But I enjoy it. I especially like playing at the unassuming country course across the road from me. I'm sure the stories emerged from all the thinking I do as I play, sometimes alone, on that rugged and hilly, unaristocratic, and unforgiving course.

In a sense, these stories are a game of golf. Read these 18 tales and you will have played a round. At the same time, you will have made a tour of the planets, as old theologies recommend. You will have met the "hazards" of life and maybe even accomplished the miracle of a hole in one.

I don't want to explain it all away, but let me say that the phrase *hole in one* reminds me of the Zen circle representing the fullness of whatever has been completely emptied. A game seems empty, from a certain point of view. It is a waste of good time. Adult men and women chase a tiny ball around heaps of earth and occasional absurdly cultivated "greens." All the while, they could be doing something productive. But from a spiritual point of view, this emptiness is precious.

Just think about that hole in the ground, the object of the chase. Like a kiva. An emptiness in the earth. The empty tomb. A portal to the underworld. A goal that is nothing. Like waiting for Godot. Like sitting at meditation. Like being open to life.

What metaphors! And how wonderfully Zen! After writing this I feel that maybe I should work less and play golf more.

CHAPTER 1

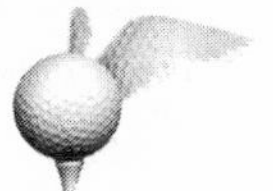

Holes in One

Shrieks of happiness drifted up the stairway from the basement to the kitchen where Roy and Dale were carefully preparing the extra large pizza that would be the penultimate culinary delight of their son's ninth birthday party.

"I hope he likes his gift," Roy said. He slipped a slice of pepperoni into his mouth before deftly scattering the pieces across the pizza like a Las Vegas dealer delivering a fateful hand of cards.

"Of course he will," said Dale.

Roy and Dale had been named by their respective parents after the singing cowboy couple who to them represented clean-cut values and style. Somehow they had found each other and had given in to what fate had ordained.

Dale was replacing a pitcher of Kool-Aid in the refrigerator when she stopped cold with the door half open. "What's that sound?"

"That's no sound," Roy answered. "That's silence."

Cautiously, they descended the basement stairs. The children were playing a game of golf using the plastic clubs and balls that had come with the set Roy had given his son, Simon, as a special gift. Roy and Dale watched as Simon putted the ball. The basement floor pitched toward the center drain like a roulette wheel, spinning luck and disaster in all directions. But the ball made an unexpected turn at the last second and dropped into the hole in the top of the slanted "green" that had come with the golf set. The children uttered a collective and rather mournful, "Oh."

"What's happening here?" Roy asked Simon's freckled, red-haired friend Daisy.

"He keeps making holes in one," she pouted. "The rest of us can't get under six."

Simon was a nerd in the making, and his sports-loving father had thought that any sport, even golf, might give his son some swagger. Still, Roy wondered, could it be that he's good at something physical?

Dale and Roy watched for 20 minutes while Simon made one hole in one after another and all of his friends tried hard to break ten.

"Let me try that," Roy finally said. He had been a golfer since he was six and played an average of twice a week with a handicap of 12. He grabbed the short plastic putter and sighted the hole from several angles. Then he made his skillful shot. It missed by several inches and shot toward the basement wall on the far side of the room. Roy settled for 11.

He handed the putter to Simon, who made yet another spectacular hole in one, bouncing off first the furnace and then a bicycle tire.

Dale, who wore her motherhood like a 1940s apron around her pudgy waist, clapped her hands. "Who wants cake? Come on upstairs!" She called out, thus breaking the tension created by the father-and-son competition.

The next day Roy took Simon to a nearby miniature golf course, where Simon shot 18 on the 18-hole course. Roy finished with a less noteworthy score of 56.

"Where did you learn to play like that?" Roy asked his son in the car on the way home.

Simon thought for a moment. "Nowhere. It just feels completely natural."

"We'll have to try it out on a real golf course," said Roy. "Are you up for that?"

"I'll give it a try," Simon answered solemnly, "but, since I just started playing, I can't promise anything."

The next day father and son went to the nearest course, which was a short one, mostly par threes and a few par fours. Simon did the nine-hole course in nine, while his father managed a skillful 44.

"Can you show me your swing?" Roy asked Simon.

"I don't know what to show you. I aim for the hole on the green. Isn't that how you do it?" Simon showed no cockiness but spoke with utter innocence.

"That's what I do, too," said the father. "But I don't get the ball in the hole every time."

They decided to play another nine holes on the small course, and this time Roy asked his friend and sometime golf partner Fred to join them. On the fourth hole Fred muttered something that sounded like an obscenity and walked off the course. At the snack bar later on he told Roy that his son must be cheating somehow.

"How could he cheat?" Roy glanced over at Simon, who was sipping lemonade. "He's using my old bent-out-of-shape clubs. He never gets in the rough or a bunker, so there's no way he can break the rules or do anything we can't plainly see."

"He has to be cheating," Fred said. "There's no other explanation short of divine intervention."

"I know this kid," Roy answered. "There's nothing mystical about him."

Simon became a celebrity at the miniature golf centers and grew up with a considerable amount of local fame. When Simon was 14 Roy went to talk to the pro at the local country club about him. Lorenzo had once been on the professional circuit and knew more about golf than anyone else around. Roy explained the phenomenon of his son and golf. Lorenzo laughed. "Why make a joke at your son's expense?"

"It's no joke," said Roy. "Look, why don't you play with us on the country club course."

"No," said Lorenzo. "You know as well as I do that you have to be almost professional to break 90 on this course. You'll only discourage the kid."

"You don't understand," said Roy. "I haven't seen Simon miss a shot yet."

"All right," said Lorenzo, "but if it goes bad, I'll want to cut the game before it's finished. Deal?"

"Deal," said Roy.

The next day the three showed up for an early-morning tee time. Lorenzo shook Simon's hand and wished him luck. "If things don't go well, no worries," he said. "We'll stop the game and try another time."

"I don't know," said Simon. "I've never played on a real course. I think I should take some lessons."

"You should be giving the lessons," said Roy with a wink.

Lorenzo teed off first and hit his ball about 275 yards. The ball started low and then rose into the sky and arced down on a trajectory fairly in line with the green. It was a great shot.

Roy went next, wagging rather excessively when he addressed the ball. He had never played with Lorenzo before and he was nervous. The ball popped up high and short and landed in the middle of the fairway about a hundred yards on.

Then it was Simon's turn. He stood up at the tee and swung the heavy driver in practice as though it were a ball and chain. "Where's the green?" he asked, looking worried.

"It doglegs to the right and sits up right behind that grove of trees. You can't see it from here," his father answered.

"I can't hit the ball if I can't see the green," Simon said with a frown.

"In golf you can't always see the green from the tee box," said Lorenzo.

"Just hit the ball and curve it behind those trees," said Roy.

Simon swung clumsily at the ball, topped it, and watched it spin like a World War II spitfire that had received enemy ammo up its tail. It went about 15 yards. He proceeded to hit the ball in a series of 15-yard advances until he reached the green in 25 strokes. His father was red in the face.

"Are we here for a lesson?" Lorenzo asked.

"Let's try the next hole," his father said. "Maybe Simon's nervous."

The next hole was a par three, 175 yards. Lorenzo's ball veered to the left and landed in a sand trap in front of the green. Roy's veered to the right and landed in the other trap. Simon let loose a swing, the grace of which Lorenzo had never seen before. The ball bounced a foot in front of the green and rolled into the hole.

"I've never heard of a hole in one on this hole," said Lorenzo. "Congratulations, Simon." He shook Simon's hand. "What a stroke of luck!"

"Just wait," said Roy. "This isn't about luck."

Simon and Lorenzo each holed out for three on the hole and then walked to the next tee, a par four, 350 yards. Lorenzo grabbed Simon by the shoulders and pointed toward the green.

"See that big maple tree on the right? Aim for that and you'll avoid the water that is hidden from view here."

Simon shrugged.

Lorenzo hit his ball awry with a massive swing and spun it far left into the neighboring fairway. Roy hit his up into the sky again about 50 yards. Simon stood at the tee, wishing for a good shot.

"Is that the green?" he asked, pointing straight ahead.

"That's it," said Lorenzo. "Don't try too hard. It will be great if you get on the green in four strokes."

Simon stood at the ball and created another magnificently smooth and graceful swing that sent the ball on a perfectly straight path toward the green. At first, it looked as though the ball would stay low and hit the maple tree. But then it soared and disappeared from sight.

"Good hit!" shouted Lorenzo.

It took a while for Lorenzo to find his ball. He hit his second shot just short of the green, while Roy got on in two. When all three arrived at the green, Lorenzo began looking for Simon's ball.

"You hit that thing a mile," he said, "and I don't know how you did it. Smoothest damn swing I've ever seen. But it must have faded. I don't see it anywhere."

"Look in the hole," said Roy.

"No," said Lorenzo, but he looked anyway and pulled the ball out, noting carefully Simon's signature three-dot triangle on the ball. "But . . ." he said.

The invisibility of the green was Simon's Achilles' heel and he took lessons for the long holes with doglegs. If it weren't for that, he would have been winning golf tournaments everywhere. As it was, he hit numerous holes in one in every game he played, but his score rarely drew him even close to winning.

His blind game improved somewhat and his sighted game lost none of its magic. People came to watch him play and learned to skip the holes where he couldn't see the green.

He was 21 and headed for a career in engineering when one day on a golf course, surrounded by a curious and slightly antagonistic crowd, a young woman tugged at his sleeve. She was so beautiful she looked airbrushed. She wore the pastel colors of commercial purity and her teeth were white and perfectly formed.

"I think I can help you," she murmured. "With the doglegs."

"Talk to me when the game is over," Simon said patiently. The game ended quickly and Simon came in with a score of 123 for 18. He never did learn how not to top the ball on doglegs.

They sat at an intimate table set near the white picket fence in a corner of the garden outside the clubhouse.

"I'm in charge of A/V in my sorority house," she said with enthusiasm and authority. "I've watched your career."

"Or the lack thereof," said Simon.

"And I think I have a solution."

"As you can imagine," said Simon, "I've been offered a great many solutions. None of them has worked."

"Have you tried a video camera that feeds back pictures of the green to a screen at the tee?"

"Is it legal?"

"I have found no references to such a setup in the rule book."

"Which was written before video cameras existed," added Simon.

"So?"

"All right, let's give it a try."

The girl's name was Gloria and she was glorious indeed. The apparatus worked on the first try. Simon looked into a small screen on a compact video camera receiving an image from another camera at the green. He kept his eye on the screen as he swung back his driver, and the smooth arc returned to his swing. The ball launched like a moon rocket and curved at the appropriate places and landed on the green and then dropped into the hole.

"Gloria," Simon asked after conquering his first dogleg. "How can I repay you?"

"You can marry me," Gloria said.

And Simon agreed.

They married and had twins and made a lot of money on the golf tour.

One day in the seventh year of their marriage Simon said to Gloria, "I'm not happy with the video setup. It's artificial. I'm manufacturing my swing. I'm no longer a natural."

"You know, Simon," Gloria replied, "the camera and I were a team from the very beginning. No camera, no glory."

So they divorced. Incidentally, the twins did not have the gift.

Simon went back to losing tournaments and, for the most part, being happy. He was still making holes in one at the majority of holes but his score on the other holes, the doglegs, was so high that he never won. The crowds following him went back to skipping the doglegs or booing him mercilessly. Something about the booing satisfied Simon.

Then one day, just after he hit a spitfire 50 yards from the tee and the crowd comforted him with some unusually fervent boos, a woman tugged at his sleeve.

"I think I can help you," she said.

At lunch in the garden of the clubhouse, she leaned close and whispered the magic word. Visualization.

"You can visualize the green, and once you learn to do it as though you are actually seeing it with your eyes, you will be able to hit your magic balls. I'll teach you."

Simon was ready to return to glory without any technological assistance, and Mona's visualization idea seemed like the ideal solution.

"What do you want in return?" he asked cautiously.

They were married within a month. Every day Mona gave Simon lessons in visualization. She taught him how to imagine the invisible green so sensuously and so vividly that it impressed itself panoramically on his retina, albeit virtually, and he could commence his Jell-O smooth swing and find the hole on every dogleg. "I'm back," he announced to the world.

His next year on the tour he played ten games in 180 strokes. No other golfer came close to him. He won millions of dollars, a feat that made him many enemies and drew crackpots to him like flies to molasses.

Late one night, as he was locking his car in front of his 20,000-square-foot home, a particularly sleazy fan scuttled out from behind a large rhododendron and hissed, "Tell me the scam."

"Scam?" howled Simon. "Does the ball not go in the hole? Am I using magnetic clubs? Are there mirrors set in the traps directing the ball to the hole? Scam? There is no scam."

"What's the secret?" a local sports announcer and journalist asked him, again late at night, popping out from behind the same rhododendron. "How do you do it?"

Simon told the announcer that he did it with a camera embedded in his occipital lobe, and the announcer believed him, writing about it in the newspaper's weekend edition. Golfers the world over began petitioning surgeons to give them a photomechanical insert, but the doctors only disabused the public of their wishful demands with threats of brain injury.

Finally, a reporter from *Newsweek* got the idea to ask Simon's wife for the secret. After being guaranteed a certain income for life, Mona relented. "Visualization," she said simply—one of the most expensive words ever spoken.

So everyone began visualizing and offering seminars and master's classes on it. Mona became rich in her own right and divorced Simon. He began to see his golf talent and lack thereof as a stain on his life. One day he took his clubs and tossed them in the pond he had had built behind his house. Golf had ruined him.

But as every serious golfer knows, golf is not a game; it's a psychological affliction. It tells you when it has had enough of you, not vice versa. It's the 800-pound gorilla; you're the weak kid on the beach. It's a psychosis, and you're the patient.

Simon whistled in the dark for a year, pretending that golf had no claim on him. He tried to live as though he had never swung a seven iron before and had never felt the spring of moist bent grass under his feet. He persisted in this delusion until the emptiness in his life screamed like a banshee from hell.

He went to a psychiatrist who chatted with him meaninglessly for weeks before the golf complex emerged.

"I was certain it had to be a woman," the psychiatrist moaned.

"No, it's golf," Simon confessed.

"Your father was an avid golfer."

"Yes, and why are golfers always called avid?"

"And golf influenced your childhood."

"Defined it."

"And led to a marriage."

"Shotgunned me into two."

The psychiatrist raised an eyebrow. "Nothing in medical literature suggests anything psychoneurotic about golf."

"A simple lacuna," Simon observed.

"It's in the family of origin."

"You wouldn't say, 'He's an avid typist.'"

"There's only one thing to do. Go into it. Face the demon. Play golf."

Simon's return to golf had cost him several hundred dollars a week with the psychiatrist, who assured Simon that it was worth every penny.

He went back to his unfortunate and unfulfilling pattern of holing-in-one all holes but doglegs. It was maddening, clinically. One day he noticed a pretty and rather distracted woman in the midst of the crowd who had gathered to watch his demise at the dogleg. When the usual hisses and catcalls died down he waited—and waited—but she never approached him. He tracked her down after the round.

"I couldn't help notice that you didn't do anything," he said rather sadly. "You have nothing to offer me? No help? No advice?"

"Nothing," she said.

"What's your name?"

"Moon."

"Oh God," Simon let slip.

"You don't like it, call me Luna. That's how I was baptized."

"How about Night Object?" Simon offered.

"I find that acceptable." She smiled.

"Do you have any suggestions for my game?" he asked.

"No. You don't need any."

"But I lose all the time."

"So?"

"Do you want to get married?"

"No."

"Do you visualize?"

"What?"

"What would you do if you were me and were losing every game of golf in spite of hitting holes in one all over the place?"

"I'd hit the ball to the green even though I couldn't see it. Golf takes a little faith."

"Do you think faith takes a little golf?"

"That's why I'm here."

Simon proposed to Luna and they were married one year later—after Simon's game improved to the point where he could hole doglegs.

They lived in a modest house and he played on the pro circuit with modest success. He was taking out the trash one evening when a reporter from the local newspaper approached him. He asked him the secret to his game and said he would not tell anyone and would never write about it.

"All right," Simon responded. "Here's the secret. Hitting a golf ball is like putting a teaspoon into a cup of tea. You never miss the cup, do you?"

"As a matter of fact, no," the reporter said, who was now writing madly in his tiny spiral notebook. "Can you expand on that?"

"There's nothing more to say. It's the secret to the whole thing. I've never uttered it before tonight. You have the exclusive claim on it. I will deny I ever said it, but you now know the whole story in sordid detail."

"I'm not sure what I know," the reporter said, hoping to egg Simon on.

But Simon was not to be egged. For the first time since he was a child he felt free. He had no gift; he was like everyone else.

"Can you teach this to anyone else?" the reporter persisted.

"Yes, it would take about three seconds."

"And then would your student be able to make every hole?"

"A bit redundant, but yes. There's no reason why he wouldn't. He'd have my secret. The only thing is, he'd have to know it when he swung. Maybe that's where the skill comes in."

"Would you teach me?"

"I already have."

"How did you solve the problem of not seeing the green?"

"I learned how to put a spoon in a cup with my eyes closed. Easy. But it took me half a lifetime and three marriages to think of it."

CHAPTER 2

Golfitis

Abe Robinson made his living by helping people create businesses. He had received his M.B.A. through a correspondence course that required him to spend most of his college years online. As each hour passed, during which he learned a little business law and a little economic theory, he pictured his reward as having a comfortable home, a near-perfect family, and a life of relative ease. Such an outcome would make all his study worthwhile.

The reality was rather different. People came to him with outlandish ideas for bizarre businesses and they always expected immediate and extravagant success. They placed all their confidence in Abe to maneuver a way through the laws and banks and warehousing and shipping options and come up with a smooth-running operation.

When Abe returned home every evening on the commuter line that stopped in his little town, he was noticeably more nervous than when he left in the morning. His wife, Meryl, pointed this fact out to him twice a day: once in the morning and once at night, a regularity that seemed to aggravate Abe's condition.

One evening Meryl sat Abe down in his tiny den. "Abe," she said, "you're becoming a nervous wreck. Your job is killing you."

Abe's shoulders sank a few inches. Since he'd began his career in earnest, his torso had changed—permanently—so that his shoulders now sloped at a steep angle down from his neck. "It isn't the job qua job," Abe said.

Meryl took on the impatient look she always did when he peppered their conversation with Latin. He had majored in medieval philosophy as an undergraduate. His knowledge of Latin was considerable, but it didn't help him as much in his law studies as he had hoped. "It's the people I have as clients. They're nuts. Their ideas don't make sense. And they're unreasonably demanding."

Meryl looked at him with a mixture of sympathy and loathing. "Have you considered a different occupation?"

"Meryl," Abe pleaded, "what can I do? Not many companies are looking for someone with a degree in medieval philosophy. I'm doing what my master's degree qualifies me for. You want me to open a pet shop?"

Abe's tendency toward non sequiturs inflamed Meryl. She saw it as a defense against self-disclosure. Over the years she had attended several lectures on psychology and prided herself on her analytical acumen. "I have a suggestion," she said in the tone of a drill sergeant trying to be helpful. "Why don't you take up a sport or a hobby? Your Uncle Finbar was a stamp collector, and he was always serene. And he was a city bus driver."

"I hate stamps. I hate collecting. I'm not athletic. I hate sports."

Meryl got specific. "I bought you a membership in the Upstate Country Club and arranged for you to have golf lessons," she said with muscle in her voice.

"You what?" cried Abe, lifting his sunken shoulders an inch. "I hate golf. Membership in a country club is expensive. We can't afford it."

"We can't afford not to do something. Golf will help you relax. A lot of men do it."

"A lot of men twist their clubs around their golf partners' necks, too. The game is notorious for making people frustrated and angry."

"That is actually a benefit of the game," said Meryl, pouncing on to Abe's line of thought "The anger and frustration are obviously out of proportion to the stress of a game. Golf allows symbolic expression of otherwise repressed emotions." She paused. "The point is, Abe, it's a done deal. You are a member. And I know you won't want to waste the money we have spent signing you up."

"I hate golf," Abe said, but Meryl was already heading to the kitchen to prepare dinner. "And now you're going to see what happens when I get trapped into doing something I hate!"

On the following Saturday Abe went to the country club to see, first, if he could get out of the membership, and second, if release was impossible, to see how bad golf lessons could be. His instructor was a brilliant white smile attached to a cardboard-cutout face. The man must have been 21, of perfect weight, perfect height, and perfect manner. Abe could find no fault with him, and that was an achievement for Abe, who could spot human frailty like an eagle spying on a rabbit at 75 feet. Still, Abe found the young man's perfection slightly nauseating.

Abe expected Norm, the golf pro, to take him out to the practice putting green and torture him with an hour of putting small balls into impossibly small holes. Instead, Norm took him to the pro shop and showed him their wide selection of golf bags. The beauty of the bags caught Abe by surprise. He told Norm to leave him alone for a while as he selected the one that suited him. He particularly liked a large leather-trimmed affair with many side pockets and a velvet fabric. The price tag was rather shocking. But this was all Meryl's idea. Better to put it into a golf bag than into a psychiatrist's pocket.

"Of course, you'll need some clubs to go into that bag," Norm said when he returned. It took the rest of the afternoon for Abe to select a basic set of irons and woods. Better to spend the time now and be prepared, he thought. Good equipment is essential—he knew this much about golf—to be able to play well and not get discouraged.

"How did it go?" Meryl asked on his return.

"Fine," Abe said. "We didn't have time to play, but I got acquainted with the basics—equipment and that sort of thing. I'm going back next Saturday for my first real lesson."

Abe looked relaxed and Meryl was pleased to see Abe's positive attitude. Still, there was something . . . she struggled to define it . . . something slightly unsettling about her husband's easy manner.

The next Saturday Abe purchased several boxes of golf balls, a rather nice diamond-studded ball marker, a divot repair tool made of platinum, and a visor once worn by President Eisenhower. Abe was astonished at the condition of the relic. It didn't have a smudge on it. Ike probably never broke a sweat at golf, given his experiences on D-day.

Norm asked him to take a few practice swings with a new driver that had just come in. Abe had never held a driver before. He loved the balance and weight of the new club and ordered one for himself. Going out to the tee, he realized that the golf bag he had bought was too heavy for a single person to lift, so he asked about a lightweight version.

On the tee, Abe also noticed that the golfers around him were dressed in stylish clothes, from cleated wing-tip cordovan-colored shoes to beautifully draped short-sleeve Cuban-style shirts that showed no wrinkles and no rings of sweat. Attired in his regular weekend fashion disasters, Abe couldn't walk fast enough back to the pro shop. After all, a member had to look good.

But his new navy-colored wicking polo shirt and the argyle sweater-vest only accentuated his collapsing shoulders. Norm looked him up and down and said sadly, "You can't play golf with shoulders like that, Abe. The club has a fitness room, and members get a discount. I suggest we start there and lift those shoulders up."

"Sweater-vest?" Meryl said when Abe got home from the club.

"I felt chilly."

"How was the lesson?"

"No lesson yet, but Norm assures me that we'll start next week."

The next week, Abe indeed began lessons in earnest. On the driving range Norm showed him how to line up the ball, keep his head down, swing the club at the proper angle, and follow through and release from his swing. Abe tried to remember the order of these requirements, but he didn't have much of a head for body language.

When Abe returned home later that morning, he found Meryl hunkered down in her massive wingback chair with a wad of papers spilling from her hands.

"Do you know how much money you've spent on golf so far? It's in the thousands of dollars."

"It was your idea," Abe said calmly, lifting his shoulders a tad.

"And you just started playing the game today," Meryl went on at a higher pitch.

"Actually," Abe said, "I hope to play a real game next week. I was at the driving range today. But Norm says my arc is good."

"Your arc should be plenty good for the amount of money you're paying him alone."

"The way I look at it," Abe said with unnatural equanimity, "it's better to pay Norm than a bunch of doctors who can't help me and cost much more in the long run. *Esse est percipi.* It's better to see my improvement than just talk about it and measure it."

Meryl just glared at him.

Once Abe's lessons got underway in earnest, and he began to actually play the course, he developed quickly into a decent player. He soon found a few golfing partners just a shade better at the game than he, and he set up a schedule of 18 holes twice a week. At the end of each game, he checked out the pro shop to look at any new gear or attire that may have come in. He was looking for a good left-handed glove. He had already bought a few hybrid clubs, a seven wood, and some extra wedges to give him versatility on the course.

"I have to say," Meryl admitted one Tuesday evening, just after Abe returned from the club, "you are looking more relaxed."

"That was a great idea you had, Meryl." Abe stood tall and straight. "I'm going to take the game more seriously and play three times a week. With the membership, I can play as often as I want."

"Don't overdo it," said Meryl. "Too much of a good thing . . ."

"Quidquid recipitur secundum modum recipientis," Abe said obscurely.

With the lengthening summer evening Abe was now playing golf three times a week, and was spending a considerable sum keeping his gear and his attire more than up to standards.

"Abe," Meryl admonished when he came home at 9 P.M. one evening. "Bernie Levin called the house, looking for you."

"Levin?" Abe looked blank.

"The self-cleaning fish tank business," Meryl prompted. "He called three times."

"Tomorrow," Abe said. "I'm feeling relaxed. I played such a great game—"

"You're too relaxed," Meryl declaimed. "Golf is half of your life."

"Oh, Meryl, I'd like to make it the whole of my life. I love the game."

Meryl looked flabbergasted. "Do you have the stuff to be a pro?"

"No," Abe said with a dejected frown, "and I never will. The slope in my shoulders keeps my back from being in the proper angle at contact."

That night Meryl calmed herself with the belief that psychologically Abe had gone too far in the opposite direction and would naturally find the center pretty soon. At least that was her hope. But Abe began playing golf every day of the week and was losing clients. For all practical purposes he had given up his job, and their savings were close to being used up.

"All I want to do is play golf," Abe said, when Meryl told him about yet another client who threatened to sue. "It's your fault. You talked me into this."

"All right," shouted Meryl, "it's my fault. And here's what you are going to do about it. I've heard of a psychologist who works with people addicted to games and sports. I've made an appointment for you. Tomorrow."

The next morning Abe took an elevator to the 72nd floor of a new skyscraper in a new suburban development of shopping centers, condos, and offices. Dr. Rogers's office was stunning with contemporary paintings in soothing blues and grays on the walls, sleek furniture, and unnatural quiet, due to special soundproofing of the walls. Sebastian, as he preferred to be called, spoke slowly and quietly. He'd created an inventory, a test for people addicted to sports.

"Mr. Robinson, I have a version I've adapted for golfers. Do you mind if I ask you a few questions?"

"Anything," said Abe, his shoulders slumped. "All I can think about is golf. It means more to me than life itself."

Dr. Rogers ignored Abe's confession. "Which iron or club is your favorite?"

"I have to think about that," said Abe. He rubbed both eyes with his fingers. "The seven iron. Yes, the seven iron is my favorite. I wish I had it here with me now."

"You can borrow mine," Dr. Rogers said, taking a club from his closet. "I keep a spare set nearby," he explained when he saw Abe's look of surprise.

"Why the seven iron, do you think?" Abe asked, comforted by the familiar weight now in his lap.

"Seven is a favorite number of many people. It's a number of luck, good fortune, health, and happiness."

"Yes," said Abe. "Medieval philosophy understood it as four plus three: wholeness plus perfection. I never made the connection."

"It's also a club," Dr. Rogers went on, "an instrument of aggression: blunt, ancient, basic, and dangerous."

Abe gripped the seven iron with both hands as if to try out Dr. Rogers's hypothesis. "You think I have hidden anger? My wife thinks that, too."

"Another question," Dr. Rogers said, ignoring Abe's comment. "Do you prefer getting the ball in the hole or hitting it from the tee?"

"I can tell that these are revealing questions. Very professional."

"And your answer?"

"Definitely the hole. I love the sound of the ball bouncing around in the hole. I like putting my fingers in and . . . oh, oh. I think I know what you're going to say."

"It's not what you think, Abe. It's all rather simple: you prefer not to hit from the tee because your aggression is repressed, but you like to fiddle with the hole as an indirect expression of your anger. Not being aggressive on the tee betrays the fact that you are angry. Do you understand? In psychology we often deal with the principle that everything is backwards twice."

"I need help. I understand that," said Abe.

Dr. Rogers wrote something on a piece of paper and handed it to Abe. "This is the address of a group that meets one evening each week. I've never been there, but from what I've heard, it may help you. If it doesn't, come back for some medication."

"A medication for golf addiction?"

"Just come back, Abe."

Two evenings later Abe went in search of the meeting. He couldn't find a building with the address that Dr. Rogers had given him, but he did find two buildings with numbers on each side of the one he was given. When he arrived at the supposed meeting place, all he found was a parking lot. He was about to go back home, when he heard voices toward the back of the lot. He investigated and came upon a group of about 20 people, men and women, sitting on the ground in a circle.

"Are you looking for us?" said a woman with a blue bandana on her forehead.

"Maybe. My name's Abe."

A man spoke up. "We're the country's first support group for golf addiction," he said. "We think of ourselves as GA, Golfers Anonymous. Are you a sick golfer, Abe?"

Abe felt cornered. "De gustibus non est disputandum," he said.

"Do you speak English?" a haggard-looking man asked.

"All right. I admit it," Abe said. "I am a sick golfer. I can't control myself. I can't stand it when I don't have a club in my hands."

Several people nodded. They knew exactly what he was talking about.

"And golf has destroyed your life," someone yelled out.

A man in a dirty suit walked up to Abe. "We meet like this because we can't find a place. We are the most despised of despised groups. We are the lepers of humankind," he moaned. "Would you like to join us?"

Panicked, Abe backed away from him. "I have to go and see my doctor. He has something for me."

"A cure?" someone cried out as he hurried back to his car. "Have they found a cure?"

Dr. Rogers managed to fit Abe in just after his 2 P.M. session ended. "It's a muscle shot," he explained as he prepped the syringe.

"Ouch," said Abe.

"They're actually thinking of naming the disease 'golfitis,'" Dr. Rogers said. "No doubt it has a genetic base."

"Then what can I do? Is my life over?"

"Not at all. I think we should also try the psychoanalytic approach. Don't try to overcome your problem, but go deeper into it. Arrange your life so you can play, say, 9 holes every other day, 18 on weekends and holidays, and then visit me once a week to reflect on your experience. I think that will do the trick."

So Abe arranged to play daily, see his doctor, and go back to work.

One fall evening Meryl studied his face and his body posture and said, "Abe, to tell you the truth, I didn't think it would work. But you're looking great, and we've paid off half our debts and you're working regularly again. And you're not nervous."

Abe chuckled. "Yup, it was touch and go for a while. But now I'm back to golf qua golf, not just a neurotic version of the game."

As Meryl passed by his chair, he pressed the large-print novel he was reading close to his chest.

"Abe?"

He pulled a golf catalog free from the pages of the novel. "They have a sale on balls you can track with a kind of radar," he said sheepishly.

CHAPTER 3

The Affair of the Pitching Wedge

Mary Carter's life began to fall apart on a Wednesday morning in late May when her friend Sharon invited her for a round of golf. Mary had never played before, but Sharon was a persuasive person, and anyway she had been looking for a diversion that would be both healthy and social. The first game was set for the following Wednesday. Mary had two lessons before then and when she arrived at the course to meet Sharon she could tell the difference between a wood and a wedge.

Her first drive was not auspicious, but at least it didn't roll along the ground or bounce off a tree or shank off to the side. It was a respectable, if not long, nudge toward the green and to the edge of the fairway. A row of pine trees, hungry for golf balls, edged the boundary line but kept their distance from Mary's innocent and attractive ball.

Getting onto the green, she found, was the hard part. She hit from one side of it to the other, all grounders, until sheer exhaustion directed her closer to the hole. Putting, too, was a mystery. The ball should fall in easily, but somehow—wind or the tilt of the earth on its axis—kept it from making that wonderful sound, a sort of ringing thud, that golfers dream about.

The second hole was better, and Mary gained confidence and had thoughts of playing another game someday. The third brought a challenge that hadn't come up in her lessons on the driving range: a water hazard. Her drive rolled speedily along the ground until it came to a stop in front of a swampy lake big enough to have the wind whip up whitecaps. She was supposed to hit over that near-ocean of water and make her way to the green, which was placed on top of a faraway hill. She began to consider this the first and last golf game of her career.

Sharon taught her how to hit around the lake, albeit adding several strokes to her score, and to tack her way up the hill to the green. In a matter of a half hour, she finished the third hole. She was taking a swig from a bottle of water when a rugged-looking man, carrying a bag with just a few clubs, walked onto the green. He appeared happy—in charge of himself and his game. Mary wondered at his optimism.

"Mind if I play through?" he said politely and engagingly.

"Join us," said Sharon, to Mary's dismay. She didn't want some man watching her massacre the game, the course, and her pride.

"Golf is the perfect game," Jack said, as the threesome walked toward the next green. "Raw nature all around, the weather in your face, people to meet and talk to, exercise, the challenge of technique, the romantic history of the sport. You can't beat it."

Mary was soon taken by Jack's positive attitude and his heroic posture. He swung easily and gracefully, bringing his whole body into play. He seemed to enjoy every stretch of muscle. Mary hadn't learned yet that golf can bring out the guile in any person, however innocent they may be, but she could tell that Jack was like an open-face sandwich—you got what you saw and saw what you got.

"How long have you been playing?" Jack asked Mary during that first round.

"This is my first game. I took two lessons."

"I'm astonished. You're doing well. Gifted, I might say—precocious even." Mary observed that Jack was not reserved about compliments.

Jack was a golf adventurer. As soon as he hit a ball, he was off after it with a long stride. He talked a great deal, but he was always interesting, as when he remarked on how a golf ball used to be stuffed by hand and sewn inside out.

The evening of her first game, Mary sat at the dinner table and gushed to her husband, Gerry. She had finally found something to do with her life that wasn't work or service oriented, she said. Gerry didn't show equal enthusiasm, but he allowed that she had found something to do with her life. His passion was fishing, and Mary had spent many a dreary hour in their small leaky rowboat. She couldn't wait for her next game of golf. For some reason, she didn't feel like telling Gerry about Jack.

The weekend plodded by and Mary arranged to take two more golf lessons. She hoped Jack might show up at her next game but thought that was improbable, since he had joined up with her and Sharon only because he was a single. But that Wednesday as she drove into the parking lot of the club, she saw Jack with a foot up on the bumper of his BMW roadster, tying a golf shoe.

Mary parked, took out her clubs, and walked over to him.

"Hello, Jack," she said, as though she just happened to be passing by.

"Hi, there," said Jack. "You playing today?"

Mary doubted that Jack was unaware that she and Sharon played on Wednesdays. In fact, she remembered making a point to inform Jack of that arrangement.

"Why don't you join us?"

Jack straightened up with a smile. Mary noticed that even the simple act of lacing his shoes seemed to make him happy.

"Maybe the two of you would like to play by yourselves," he said.

"Oh, Jack, you know we'd love to have you play with us." Mary laughed. "Let's quit the acting."

Jack didn't protest either the invitation or the commentary.

By the back nine of their second game, Jack was giving lessons to both Sharon and Mary, though his attentions were clearly directed toward Mary, and he took every chance to embrace her from behind, place her hands on the club, and show her how to swing. Mary didn't protest the lessons but justified an innocent flirtation by actually learning something.

"I didn't expect to see Cupid on the golf course," Sharon remarked when she and Mary were packing their cars and Jack had left.

"It's just fun," said Mary. "Nothing serious. I like the way Jack plays golf."

"Sure you do," said Sharon.

At dinner that night Gerry roused himself to ask, "Where were you today? I tried calling you."

"Gerry, it's Wednesday. I was playing golf."

"With who?"

"With whom?" Mary corrected. "With Sharon, of course."

"Did you play eighteen holes?"

"Yes, I played eighteen holes. What's the interrogation for?"

"You're always home. I can count on you being here. I don't like this . . ."

"Long leash?" Mary added.

"Marv, the golf pro, told me he saw you playing with a man."

"You mean playing golf with a man. So? Half the population is male."

"You know what I mean. I know what you're up to."

"I'm glad you do, because I don't," said Mary. She had nothing to hide, but she felt uneasy. Guilty? Guilty about what? Golf with a woman friend and a man she hardly knew?

"Gerry, you're welcome to play with me. Any time." She didn't really mean it, but she thought it might be like jumping one of his checkers in the argument, if that's what it was.

"I have to work," he said, invoking the long-suffering slave. "I don't have time."

Mary found it difficult to jump that one.

The following Tuesday evening Sharon called to say that she had a doctor's appointment the next day and couldn't play golf.

"Come late," Mary suggested.

"I'll see what I can do."

The next morning Mary showed up at the first tee by herself. She looked all around for Jack, but saw only the usual crowd of sun worshippers, socialites, and those who spent more time at the clubhouse bar than on the course. Suddenly, behind her, there he was in all his ebullience.

"I guess it's the two of us today," Mary said.

"Too bad," he said, with his lower lip sticking out.

They decided to rent a cart and gaily they ripped around the course. Mary didn't worry about her score; throughout her life luck was on her side, and now, with Jack beside her, she felt open to inspiration for the lucky chip, the intuitive drive. She felt giddy in the absolute freedom and pleasures of the course—in the open space and the pleasures of the game.

At the eleventh hole she spotted Gerry. He was hunched over the steering wheel of a cart and driving fast over bunkers and around islands of trees and bushes. He looked like a demonic child from a horror movie.

He drove up to them as they were both about to chip onto an elevated green. He stayed in the cart and fumed at them with an enormous frown that appeared monstrous against the beauty of the day.

"Mary," he screamed, "who is this jerk you're with?"

"Gerry," Mary said calmly. "What are you doing here? You're interrupting my game."

"Interrupting your game is right. What game are you playing, anyway?" Gerry remained in the cart shouting at Mary and gripping the steering wheel.

"Gerry, I'd like you to meet—"

"With all the available women in the world, what are you doing with my wife?" Gerry bellowed at Jack.

"I'm sorry, Jack," Mary said, embarrassed. Then to Gerry: "Gerry, go home. We'll talk there. I'm going to finish my game."

"I'll see you in the clubhouse," Gerry howled and then started his cart with a jerk and putt-putted away.

"This is awful," Mary said to Jack. "I don't know what has got into him. He's never like this."

"It's easy," said Jack. "You start living your life the way you want to. You get interested in something, and suddenly you're more attractive. He doesn't want to lose you."

They finished the game in three hours and Jack went to his BMW. Mary went to the clubhouse, where she found Gerry at the bar surrounded by shot glasses.

"All right, Gerry," she said. "Let me have it."

"I'm thinking divorce, Mary. I've had time to work it all out. You're cheating on me and I'm entitled to a divorce."

"Playing golf is cheating?"

"Playing golf with sicko there is cheating. Be honest. You're having an affair."

Mary called to the waiter and asked for an orange juice. "I've played golf with a man twice. That's an affair?"

"Golf is a sexual act," Gerry said with a bit of a slur.

"Oh, boy," said Mary. "Tell me more."

"It's pleasurable, it involves the body, usually two people do it, it takes about three hours—"

"That leaves us out," Mary interrupted.

"A little white ball goes into a cup."

"That I don't get," Mary said.

"And the clubs are obvious phallic symbols. The club goes in the bag, the ball goes in the hole, and someone always scores."

"And you call my friend Jack a jerk. This is the sickest thing I've ever heard."

"I've studied psychoanalysis, Mary. I know what I'm talking about."

"But you've never studied or even played golf. Gerry, it's an innocent sport. Jack's a golf buddy. I hardly know him. I don't even know his last name."

"Smythe," Gerry said quietly.

"How do you know that?"

"I had him investigated."

"Gerry! This is only the second time I've seen this man," Mary fumed. "You know what I think? Your jealousy—and let me tell you it's your jealousy and has nothing to do with my feelings—is bringing you to life. You're finally doing something, even if it's stupid."

"Saying endearing things isn't going to sway me."

"What—" Mary spluttered.

"Are you saying you don't love this man or like him or feel attracted to him?"

"What, do you want me to be a nun? Yes, I like him. I have a small attraction to him, to be honest. But on a scale of one to a thousand, I'd say my attraction to him is six hundred thirty-one."

"That's over five hundred!"

They sat in silence for a moment then Gerry asked. "You don't know what he does for a living, do you?" He looked as though he was about to win a move.

"No, I told you, I barely know the man. You seem to know much more about him than I do."

"He's a minister in a new kind of church. That's why he's always happy, why he can play golf on Wednesdays, and why he can spend his time teaching my wife how to swing."

"How do you know that? Have you been following us?"

"A little device in your golf bag. A powerful mic. A strong transmitter. A thing in my ear."

"You're nuts. Paranoid. Clinically insane. Here's the thing, Gerry. I've been playing golf. Golf! Not cheating. Playing golf. You're going to divorce me over golf."

"Golf is just an excuse," Gerry asserted, "to find a partner for sex."

Mary couldn't believe Gerry was talking this way. She had always believed he was sane. A little odd maybe, but officially sane. Now she wasn't so sure. They both grew quiet. Gerry had another drink. Mary had more orange juice.

"Can we forget this ever happened?" Gerry said, caving in to rationality.

"How can I?" Mary snapped. "You bug my bag, investigate my acquaintance—he's not even a friend yet—and you tell me how golf is a sexual act. I'm supposed to forget all this?"

"Look," said Gerry, as if he finally had the solution. "I'll drive up to that hole once again and ask about the weather. We'll erase the previous interaction from our memories."

"By what means? A phaser. We'll call on Mr. Spock?"

The conversation continued for another hour, when Jack returned and asked Mary if she'd like him to take her somewhere safe.

Mary gathered her clubs and followed him to his car. "Do you know that Gerry was listening in on our conversation? And he has such weird ideas about golf I think he should be examined."

Jack opened the door of his BMW and Mary climbed in and he drove her to a good hotel. He paid for a room with a credit card and told Mary he'd come for her only if she called. He gave her his card. Yes, he was a minister and doing quite well, thank you. He saw golf as part of his ministry. "I'm always finding lost souls on the course," he said. "Not you, of course. Gerry."

When he left, Mary plopped down on the bed and called Sharon and told her the whole story. Sharon found it hard to believe.

"I know," said Mary. "Golf is a funny game. It looks insignificant, even stupid, but it quickly grows in a person's life into a kind of religion. It destroys a lot of marriages, and I've never seen it help one. One thing is certain," she said, reaching for the remote and clicking her way to ESPN and the day's golfing highlights. "If I ever have to choose between golf and my husband, I know which way I'll go."

"Do you want me to come over?" Sharon asked.

"No, I'll be fine. I'll just get room service and settle in for the night." She reached for the remote and began clicking her way to ESPN and the day's golfing highlights from the Dunhill Championship.

CHAPTER 4

The Archeology of Golf

After years of nudging his shovel into the earth, Peter Staegel no longer got calluses and no longer tired of coming up with dirt or the occasional small and often insignificant find. But on this day in April, one certainly to be marked on his calendar, his shovel hit something small, hard, and brittle. It was a human hand. And in the hand was a small round object made of chalk or alabaster.

Staegel was a careful, persistent, exacting archeologist reluctant to draw any extravagant conclusions from a dig. He suspected that the find might prove to be important, but he wouldn't allow himself any premature congratulations. He left the skeleton in a local university lab and took the small stone home with him to the University of Michigan, where he was a sometimes professor of ancient civilizations. He placed the stone among hundreds of other dirty, broken artifacts in his own private museum, a well-lighted closet next to his university office.

The object lay there under glass during countless classes and consultations, and no one noticed it—until one day a young adjunct professor of anthropology came by. He was in residence at the university for a semester, teaching a course on archeology and religion, and was eager to learn anything he could from his fellow faculty members. He was a curious, you might say "nosy" visitor. He'd turn things over, look into drawers, and sometimes take out a magnifying glass.

Rider, the young visitor, was looking closely at Staegel's collection and noticed the small piece of white stone.

"What's this?" he asked, turning it around in his fingers.

Staegel looked up from the pile of graduate papers on his desk. "That? Who knows? I found it in Ireland."

"Do you mind if I look at it closely?"

"Go ahead," said Staegel.

Under the object was a card disclosing the details of its discovery—date, time, place, physical circumstances, and the person who found it.

"It was in a human hand?"

"Yes, a woman's hand. Nothing came of it. I don't know what it is. Perhaps a decorative pendant."

"It was in the Boyne River Valley."

"Yes, near the river. Not far from Knowth."

"Are these other objects in the case connected?"

Staegel didn't respond.

"From the same dig?" Rider persisted.

"Yes, the same batch. I'd say within centimeters of each other."

Rider picked up a reddish hued stone. "There's writing on this one. Ogham script."

"Gibberish," said Staegel. "From an entirely different era."

"Gowf, that's what it says," said Rider.

Staegel peered at Rider from the circle of yellowish light cast by his desk lamp. "How do you know that?"

"I studied Ogham long ago."

"What does it mean?"

"I don't remember. Beat . . . slap or strike . . . something like that . . ."

"You can have it," said Staegel, returning to his papers.

"The Boyne was a place of intense ritual activity," said Rider. "I'll bet this piece has something to do with that. Could be priceless!"

"Well, good luck to you . . . If you get a price, tell me about it."

Nathaniel "Nate" Rider had studied anthropology after seeing *Raiders of the Lost Ark*. He had the adventurer's psychological makeup and saw his life work as a novel or a film, an action thriller. Staegel could spend his life in a library, but Rider longed to go after the "ark" in exotic lands, preferably accompanied by exotic women.

He did some quick research in the U of M library, and when spring break arrived he took a flight to Chichén Itzá on the Yucatán Peninsula. He stopped off at Cancún for a two-day rest to prepare himself for the adventure. In the bar of the Grand Aztec Hotel he saw a tall, incredibly vital-looking woman who seemed alone, no doubt waiting for the appearance of a man just like Rider.

"So, what are you doing here?" she asked, after having accepted a drink from the enthusiastic anthropologist. She wore a crisp, stylish safari outfit, accented with a white silk scarf that showed off her blond hair.

"I have made a find that could solve one of the great mysteries of the century," Rider said with his usual distaste for modesty. He looked to see if she was impressed and, gratified, went on.

"We have found a small round stone, clutched in the hand of a woman who walked the earth thousands of years ago." He looked again to measure the impact of his words. He had no pangs of conscience about the word *we*, since he had, after all, found the object neglected in Staegel's collection. "You aren't by any chance an archeologist, are you?" he said. "I could use an assistant or partner. This could be a revolutionary project. It could change the way we see the world."

"I'm in cosmetics," she said. "I'm developing a line made entirely of organic materials, but highly sophisticated. I expect it to transform the industry and change the way women look."

Rider realized that although their specialties appeared to be miles apart, temperamentally they were made of the same cloth.

"Close enough," said Rider. "Why don't you come with me to Chichén Itzá?"

"I need one more day in Cancún," Diana said. "A contact is bringing me a berry, the seeds of which—when crushed—create a blue that is simply dazzling."

It didn't bother Rider in the least that Diana spoke with the same consistent and unapologetic hyperbole that he himself employed. He decided to stay and get to know both Mexico and Diana a little better. In an odd little bookstore he found a volume on Mayan culture and the ball game called *ulama*. He learned that it was so dangerous that players wore protective gear. They sometimes died on the field, and in rare circumstances were sacrificed to the gods. He wondered if the game was a ritual enactment of the religious mysteries.

Chichén Itzá was a bit disappointing, but in talking with a college professor working on a dig nearby, his understanding of the serious nature of games deepened. The professor who was from Mexico City invited him to play a version of ulama with a group of archeology students. They felt that playing the game was more instructive than studying about it in a classroom. Diana, who was now part of the project, immediately volunteered to play, so Rider's ego had no choice but to say yes.

Rider wore a contraption somewhat larger than a bicycle helmet and smaller than a beekeeper's skep, but he should have worn full body armor. The ball was made of rubber strips wound tightly around a core—not unlike a golf ball, one of the students observed—and it whizzed past his head at comet speed and threatened every body part, especially the one he was hoping to bring to the foreground in his work with Diana.

A day later they hopped a plane to Costa Rica, where, Rider had heard, mysterious spheres of stone were being unearthed across the countryside. No one knew what they were for, but Rider hoped they might shed light on the meaning of the little ball he had "discovered" with Staegel. But when he saw his first Costa Rican ball, slightly larger than a basketball, he knew it couldn't have the same purpose as the one found in the woman's hand in Ireland. Costa Ricans had used them to decorate their homes, and Diana made some comment about their appropriateness for complementing certain oversized phallic images in Greece.

Some of the Costa Rican stones were admittedly smaller, about the size of a grapefruit, and several archeologists believed they may have had a ritual purpose, perhaps, like the Egyptian stone ball, an image of the sun. Maybe ulama was a game involving the Sun God and other deities. The more Rider researched, the more he was convinced that the ball in the woman's hand was a ritual object related to a sacred game.

Back in Mexico, Diana pouted. She needed to have some fun and she persuaded Rider to join her in a day of spelunking in the cenotes, open caves, and rocky ponds on the Yucatán peninsula. They were abseiling into an extravagant sinkhole when Diana glimpsed, in the beam of her headlamp, an ancient rock painting of an elongated female figure holding what appeared to be some kind of club, possibly used for hunting. At her feet was a small circular object.

"Babe Zaharias," Diana said to Rider.

"Is that a Mayan dialect?" Rider asked as he focused his light on the figure.

"No, she was a great golfer. Here she is in the middle of her swing."

Diana traced the curve of the club's knobby end for Rider.

"This is quite a discovery," Rider said.

"Could be the greatest of the century, but you'll have to vet it for me. I'll give you six percent."

Dangling above the turquoise blue water in the sinkhole, they struck a deal.

"Generous," said Rider. "I think Babe Zaharias might fetch enough for both of us."

"What about the golf angle?"

Rider's chest tightened. He held his breath, kicked back from the rock wall, and hollered, "That's the answer! The ball in Ireland is a golf ball, probably the first one."

"Sounds impressive, I think," said Diana haltingly. She wasn't completely filled in on the matter of the stone-in-hand.

Pulling themselves up and out of the sinkhole, Rider waxed on about "his" discovery. "Maybe the PGA will be interested in a lecture from me on the prehistoric origins of the game. I could have a tournament named after me."

"That was my discovery," Diana tried to remind Rider. "I'd like to have a tournament named after me."

Rider brushed her comment aside, pretending he didn't hear her. But he was worried; maybe he had met his match in Diana. He decided to be less forthcoming with her and treat her not only as a potential lover but also a competitor. Back at the hotel, he decided to contact Staegel to test out his golf theory.

"Hello," said Staegel on a crackly phone call across the gulf. "Any news?"

"Golf," said Rider, stretching out on his queen-size bed.

"What was that?" Staegel asked. "I thought you said *golf.*"

"I did," said Rider. "I think the stone ball we found might have been the world's first golf ball."

"Interesting," said Staegel. "What do you mean, *we* found?"

"You, you found," said Rider.

"What's next?" The static in the phone took over for a few seconds.

"Go public," said Rider. "See what happens. This could be colossal."

"Don't get your hopes—" The line went dead.

Well, Staegel won't get in the way, Rider thought.

Rider now had to work out a strategy that circumvented Diana and Staegel, while keeping them both in his life. He never forgot that they were treasures, too. He placed a call to the New York *Daily Gazette,* a paper with little distinction or reputation but a sizeable readership. He wanted to make a small splash that would be heard around the world.

"What do you mean?" Rider said to the reporter who answered. "This is big news. How many people in the world play golf? How many of your readers?"

More static on the phone line.

"Good," Rider said, "now listen. Nathaniel Rider discovered the world's first golf ball. Got that?"

More static.

"How do I know it's the first? Because I'm an anthropologist. Yes, yes similar to an archeologist." Rider listened to the reporter's mindless questions. "Yes, there's more," he said, "but the discovery itself is news, the biggest news you'll hear today. Golf began several thousand years before St. Andrew's in Scotland got onto the game. It was a religious ritual. You played the game in search of the gods. Golf is searching for God. For the Aztecs, the ball was the sun, the Sun God. Yes, people today are still looking for God on the golf course. They're always trying to play the best game of their lives. That's like trying to be the best person, win the game of life."

Loud squawking from the phone.

"Yes, golf today is the same game it was thousands of years ago. The sacred element is hidden, but it's there. The great thing is that I discovered the secret by finding the first ball."

Diana walked through the door to his room at that minute and Rider quickly hung up the phone.

"I've been working an angle," she said. "I'm trying to get the golf ball and cosmetics on the same page. I see incredible possibilities in that. What do you think?"

Rider took her hand and tumbled her down onto the bed. "I can see it! A billboard with our Irish lady lying on the ground grasping her golf ball. She's in the clutches of death. In the foreground is the anthropologist and a woman. She's blonde, beautiful, wearing your smart safari suit. Her makeup, so luminous, gives color to the grisly scene."

He tried to kiss her but Diana wriggled free and said, "I was thinking I could be an archeologist discovering the golf ball up in the snow-capped mountains."

"Ireland doesn't have snow-capped mountains, unless you count winter in the Wicklow hills or the Ring of Kerry. If there is going to be any discoverer on the billboard, it should be me. I found the thing."

"I thought Staegel found it."

Rider started. Had he even mentioned Staegel to her? "Staegel's not good billboard material," he said. "Besides, I'm the one who found what was a golf ball. All he found was a stone."

Diana nodded and Rider felt assured. Diana understood that kind of reasoning.

"I'm the one who went to the trouble to learn that golf is a game where you find God, for God's sake," he said.

"Big, isn't it?" said Diana.

"Very big."

Back in the States, Rider immediately contacted the CEO of the PGA, telling him about his discovery: one, that golf is far more ancient than heretofore imagined, and two, that golf always was and still is a sacred ritual game, a way through hazards and stages toward a goal impossible to name—equivalent in every respect to the goals of the major and minor religions of the world. The grandiosity of his hypothesis thrilled Rider every time he articulated it.

The PGA lost no time erecting billboards showing the ancient and desiccated hand grasping onto the stone orb. Observers had no trouble seeing it as a golf ball, given the images of lush greens and fairways that encircled the design and the logo of the Professional Golfers' Association. Invitations to speak at golf events began streaming into Rider's e-mail inbox, and he printed up a standard contract that assured him a comfortable fee and the best conditions of travel available.

The entire enterprise was to launch with a black-tie dinner at a prestigious country club on the West Coast. The PGA announced an award for the momentous discovery and Rider spent days writing his speech describing the discovery in the Boyne Valley and subsequent research into the history of sport, in particular games played with sticks and balls. He had already come to refer to the object of the dig as "Rider Woman."

When Rider entered the plush, crowded ballroom where the dinner and award were about to take place, he felt, for the first time in his life, fully convinced that he had chosen the right profession. How else would he get such recognition and wealth? But his thoughts of glory came to a precipice when he saw a man who looked a lot like Staegel at the dais talking with the CEO of the PGA. The second surprise was to see Diana walk up to the dais and put her arm around Staegel with a gesture that appeared far more than familiar. Rider had to investigate; so he approached the head table.

Staegel saw him and stretched out a hand to greet him. "Rider, isn't it a great day?"

Rider was still confused.

"I think you know my daughter, Diana," he said, squeezing her hand.

Diana gave Rider a peck on the cheek. She seemed more reserved in the situation than Rider knew her to be. Of course—she had been in on it all along.

Before Rider could ask any questions, the CEO pulled out a chair to the far left on the head table and asked him to sit down. Staegel and Diana sat next to the speaker's podium in the center of the table. The CEO sat on the other side of the podium. Rider recognized famous golfers, current and retired, sitting in the other seats.

A chaplain said grace with an amusing reference to golf, and dinner commenced. Just before dessert the CEO of the PGA stood and presented the award to Staegel.

"The golf world profoundly appreciates the patient work of Dr. Harold Staegel in deepening our understanding of the sport and showing us how ancient it truly is." Sustained applause. Staegel stood to receive the award, a bronze sculpture of a delicate hand holding a marble stone. "And," the CEO continued, "to show our appreciation I am presenting him now with a check for two million dollars to support his ongoing research."

Staegel accepted the check and addressed the audience. "Thank you for understanding the importance of my work. I want to thank my daughter, Diana, for looking out for my interests and my colleague Nate Rider for doing yeoman's work with his follow-up studies."

Rider stood to mild applause and left the ballroom. Diana followed him out. She put her hand out. "No hard feelings?"

"None," said Rider. "I've learned never to trust a woman who thinks and speaks the way I do."

"And that's why I know you will startle the world one day with a discovery all of your own," she said.

CHAPTER 5

The Four Tailors

Wet dew made a sea of crystals on the early morning course as the dedicated foursome teed off on the first hole. Mick was the first to stand in the box and loosen his ligaments and ease his self-consciousness. He stood so that the ball lined up with his left heel and the central line of his body leaned over and away from the tee at a 30-degree angle. His posture looked entirely unnatural, like a sailing ship leaning into the wind, but when he hit the ball it soared into the sky and skimmed over the trees toward the first green. He relaxed.

Ronnie, full of fidgets and quarter swings and wiggles from his derriere, was next. He looked at the ball and then toward the green and then at the ball and then toward the green, and so on until Carl was about to come at him with his five iron. Ronnie hit the ball with a nervous chop, but still it sailed toward the green in a low arc that seemed to whistle. He was close enough to the target to step away from the box with a smile.

Carl then rocked his hefty torso to the tee box and stood and surveyed the expanse of the first hole. He made as if to swing in traditional fashion and blasted the ball high into the sky. It fell halfway to the green, sputtering out once it had cleared the ozone layer.

Finally the last of the foursome danced up between the blue markers of the tee box. In his practice swings Peter stretched back like a man of plastic, hit the ball, and stretched forward in an exaggerated curve of body, like Jacques Tati of the French comedies. His ball accordingly lifted off the tee and shot away immediately to the far left toward the next fairway over and bounced and ran a good 50 yards in the wrong direction.

Bidding farewell to their comrade, the first three players headed toward the first green. Elastic man turned left to enter the faraway and strangely mist-enshrouded land of—was it hole number six? He looked around for his ball in the center of the fairway and then decided to try the green. He was getting close to the traps that bordered the sixth green when out of the mist he saw a foursome putting on soft wet grass, their balls spinning out rooster tails of water as they sped across the green. They were large men, big as hippos, with thick thighs, big snouts, and knobby foreheads. They concentrated intensely on their shots and then laughed loudly and almost obscenely as their balls dipped into the hole from whatever range they had to contend with. Their skill and speed with the putter impressed Peter.

But as he stepped onto the green, having spotted his ball on the steep slope of the undulating surface, he suddenly felt disoriented, light-headed.

"Pardon me," he said to the group when no one was putting. "My ball seems to have landed on your green."

The smallest of the four towering figures turned his head slightly and said, in a deep ba-booming voice, "You can play through."

"No he can't," said one of the others in even boomier tones. "He's seen us."

"Now you've gone and made a mess of things," said a third, in a deep, raspy basso. "What about our anonymity?"

"Look," said Peter, thinking that maybe he had walked in on a foursome of mobsters. "My ball went into the wrong fairway. I'll just return to my—"

"Sorry," intoned the fourth player, his toga-like outer gown ruffling in the breeze. "The rules of the course say that when you join a foursome on the green, you have to stay with them to the end. Why don't you take your putt? Then we'll be a fivesome."

"But this isn't my green. I'm still on the first hole. This must be—"

"Minus fourth," said the first large man, laughing.

"He's just kidding," cut in Number Four.

"It's all right," said Number One. He then turned to Peter: "Please make your putt."

"If he holes it," said Number Two, "he gets a boon. Rules apply no matter who's putting."

"I guess you're right," said Number One. He made a grand gesture with his arm toward the sky. "If you make this putt, you get a boon. You understand?"

Peter was wondering now if he had stumbled on a tournament from the nearby mental hospital. "Boon?"

"You know, a gift, a prize," said Number Three. "For this you get the power to—"

"Don't say it," cut in Number One. Then he turned quickly toward Peter. "Did you ever want to be a doctor?" he asked with mirth in his eye. They all laughed and the earth seemed to shake.

Peter bent over his ball with the putter, but then straightened up. "Who are you guys? I don't understand half of what you're saying, and your voices are all out of some tunnel or other."

"There's nothing wrong with my voice," thundered Number One.

"We're the Four Tailors," said Number Four.

"You make clothes? All four of you?"

"Sort of," said Number Three.

"In a manner of speaking," added Two.

Peter looked for a way off the green, but a thick fog obscured the edge.

"Where's the negative third tee?" asked Number One, the tallest of the four.

"You mean the fifth," said Peter.

Number Four shook his head. "We play minus holes. Backwards. And you just happened to stumble onto our green. Now the rules say that even a mortal on these holes gets the benefits of the game. You see, golf is a heavenly game. It was invented by you know who."

"I didn't know that," said Number Three.

"Well, he invented everything, didn't he?"

"Who's that?" Peter ventured.

The large men were stunned into silence.

"Let's ignore that remark," Number Four said at last.

The four tailors leaned on their clubs and watched Peter.

"You're saying I should putt away?" he asked.

"By all means," the four said in unison.

Peter stood once again over the ball, which was about 30 feet from the hole. He made a few gentle practice swings. He lifted his head to see the four were a few steps closer.

"I need space," he said.

They backed up a foot and continued to watch with great intensity.

"I get something if I make this putt. Is that right?" he asked.

"Yes," they answered like a thunderclap from the sky.

Under normal circumstances Peter would have had trouble making a putt while others were watching him. But these four bizarre men made him even more self-conscious. He breathed deeply, lifted his head, and relaxed his arms. He wiggled his shoulders. "You guys have any tips? I'm a beginner. You seem to have been playing for a long time."

"A very, very long time," said Number Three, and the three stifled their laughs until they let out a ba-booming explosion of snot and spray.

Peter made his putt and, to his delight, he easily holed it. He then watched Number One address his ball. The man was huge and his putter looked like a drink stirrer as he fanned it in front of the ball in practice swings. Then he struck it and it shot like a bullet into the hole. Peter had never seen such a putt.

"I'd love to see you use a driver," he said.

"And would you like a thunderbolt to your cosmic essence?" growled Number Four.

"Sorry," said Peter. "I was just admiring . . ."

"You may take your boon and go now," chimed Number One in sweet grandfather-clock tones. "Join your party at the clubhouse. They have finished their round with amazing success."

"But . . ." spluttered Peter.

"Go," the four tailors said in unison.

So Peter walked off the green and out into the sunshine across fairways and greens to the clubhouse. There he found his mates celebrating their amazing round.

"I know, I know," said Peter approaching them. "You had the best golf of your life."

"How did you know?" Ronnie asked.

"I was in some never-never land with some never-never people."

They were all standing at the long, highly polished dark oak bar, where old Dan the barman ranged back and forth, refilling drinks and rearranging the bowls of peanuts. He stopped and cast a suspicious eye on Peter. "What happened to you?"

"I ran into four huge monsters playing great golf."

"You ran into them? How?" Dan asked.

"I wandered onto a green that was surrounded by mist."

"Mist, eh?" Dan said. "Your friend Ronnie, here, fell over a rock out there and we think he broke his toe." Dan looked oddly at Peter, encouraging him with nods of his head to tend to Ronnie. He then shuffled away.

"What happened to you, anyway?" Carl asked as he took a swig of his lager.

"I wandered off into the next fairway and bumped into these four big guys on the green. At first I thought they were Mafia, and then I figured escapees from the mental ward."

"They were archons," said Dan from the far end of the bar.

"Ex-cons?"

With a flash of impatience, Dan picked up the remote, lowered the volume of the TV and shuffled back to the foursome. "Archons. They guard the planets and help a person become a human being at birth."

Ronnie laughed. "Either you've served too many pints or you've gone to the cellars once too often."

Dan ignored him. "They clothe the soul with flesh—in stages. Each one has a part to play. They're like angels, only much tougher."

"They said they were tailors," Peter agreed.

"Fix his toe," said Dan. He pointed to Ronnie's foot.

"What do you mean?"

"Did they give you a boon?"

Peter nodded.

"Touch his toe," said Dan.

"Whoa," said Carl.

Peter leaned over and put a finger on Ronnie's toe. "All right," he said, "I touched his toe. Now what?"

Dan nodded to Ronnie, who stood up. "Hey, it's better! I can walk on it."

"The swelling is all gone," said Mick seriously.

"The swelling had already started to go down. I noticed it," said Carl, ever the skeptic.

"Listen," said Old Dan. "The archons play their golf here because they don't have a course up there, if you know what I mean. They borrow ours but play it backward. They put a mist around themselves and no one knows they're here."

Carl and Mick both looked at Old Dan in disbelief, and Dan went to the other end of the bar to tend some new arrivals. The four men huddled.

"I think Old Dan is turning a corner," Carl whispered. "He really believes that stuff he's saying. He used to be just a good storyteller, but this . . ."

"I saw the look in his eye," Mick confirmed. "I saw that in my Uncle Theophrast just before they took him away."

"Well, I was there," said Peter, who had been quiet up to this point. "I thought those four tailors were let out for the day from the hospital nearby."

The four golfers were shaking their heads in pity as they left the clubhouse and went to their cars to pack up their clubs and go home.

"How's your foot?" Peter asked Ronnie.

"Getting better, really. No pain."

"All thanks to the ex-con," Carl, laughing, shouted from his car.

When Peter got home, his wife and two children met him at the door. "How was the game?" she asked. Little Susie, the three-year-old, ran to her father and he picked her up with his long, elastic arms.

"Strange," said Peter. "I bumped into a foursome of tailors, very odd guys. What's happening here?"

"Little Susie cut her finger. A pretty deep gash. I put gauze on it."

Just at that point Peter looked down. He'd been rubbing the gauze with his fingers. "Let Dr. Daddy see that wound," he said to his squirming daughter.

"It's all better," cried Little Susie, ripping off the gauze to reveal a fully intact, smooth, uninjured finger.

"That's the fastest job of healing I've ever seen," said Peter's wife, astonished.

"Strange," Peter said, "I played a round with these archons—"

"You played with ex-cons?"

"Where's our dictionary?" he asked. "There's a word I want to look up."

CHAPTER 6

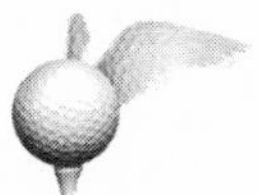

The Golf Diamond

Harry Vitrim is my neighbor now, but I knew him over 20 years ago when we were roommates in college. We were an odd couple: he the adventurer and financial genius and I the contemplative, almost antisocial one. Somehow the chemistry between us worked, and people invited us together to parties and sought out our counsel on anything from an unlikely investment of money to a romantic conundrum. We were always just good friends, even if people occasionally asked if maybe we were lovers. Harry was a dyed-in-the-wool heterosexual, and I was never drawn to Harry for anything other than friendship and companionship.

A year ago I bumped into Harry as I was entering and he was just leaving our local country club. He was carrying a gorgeous black-leather golf bag full of expensive big-name clubs, while I had my utilitarian collection of garage sale and eBay hand-me-downs. Nothing had changed about us: he had all the class, and I was the rube from the suburbs.

Harry was hurrying off to a crucial business meeting in town and he shouted that we should meet at the club for a game one day and catch up. I assumed it was one of those wishful plans that would never come to pass, but the next week we were back at the club, sitting in the luxurious lounge with the owner and one of his friends, talking about everything from the latest putting grip to local politics and business. I kept quiet, as is my custom, but Harry was at the center of the discussion, full of ideas and opinions. The topic of conversation had turned to honesty.

"In the old days I made many a good deal with a handshake and a promise," Dale, the owner of the club, was saying. "The deal was as good as your word. But things have changed, and today you need every possible contingency in writing, preferably in triplicate."

"Good business practice can't survive in the absence of trust," Harry agreed. "But it's not easy to trust even your closest friends today. Everyone is turning to private investigators to help them feel okay about their business competitors and partners. Partners!"

"I think they ought to teach business ethics more vigorously in the schools," said Vance, Dale's friend and the club's manager.

They went on in this fashion for a good half hour, when Harry mentioned that our tee time was coming up.

"You boys go and have a good time," said Dale, "and when you've finished come into the clubhouse and have a drink on me. I'll tell Joey the bartender."

We thanked him and went out to the tee box for the number one hole. Harry was a serious golfer, who always shot in the mid-80s, while I was just a duffer. I guessed he had invited me to join him because we'd been friends for so long and because he always thought of me as a special confidant.

Harry led the game off with a truly remarkable hit with his driver. The ball went medium high and straight and carried a good 200 yards. Impressive to me. I hit one much too fast and it lost its steam far short of Harry's ball. "I believe that prattle about honesty in business," Harry said as we pulled our carts along the fairway, "but it isn't always easy to put into practice. I do the best I can, but I'm not perfect."

I wondered if Harry was trying to tell me something or leading up to a discussion of something personal, but he didn't go any further with the theme, and we hit our second shots up next to the green. Harry putted out his birdie, while I hit around the green until I finally holed my bogey.

Harry had come up an economic notch or two since I last saw him. His threads were much more stylish and made of quality material, and he had several large rings on his fingers that were clearly real stones that must have cost him something. I didn't say anything, but only noticed the change. I also saw that he wore his new wealth in his style of speech and in his mannerisms. He carried his chin an inch higher than when we were in school, and he used words a little beyond the reach of his comprehension. He had always been a little jealous of my aptitude for the English language and its literature.

We were hitting our second shots on the third hole, both of us beating our way out of a sand trap, when Harry stopped. "What's that?"

I shrugged, uncertain of what he'd seen.

"That shiny thing over there." Harry walked through soft parting sand to the other edge of the trap, bent over, and picked something up.

"What is it, Harry?" I could see a sparkle in the sunlight, but the object was too small for me to make out.

"It can't be," he said softly.

"What is it?" I asked.

Carefully he placed it in the palm of my hand. At first I thought it was just a large lump of silica or sand. But on closer examination I wondered—and I knew Harry was wondering the same thing—if it was something far more precious.

Harry's expression turned to one of awe, awe qualified by greed. "I think it's a diamond," he said as I handed it back to him.

"Raw diamonds are only found in mines in Africa, I think. This doesn't look like a cut diamond, and there's no ring or necklace around. Still, if it is a diamond, someone must have lost it."

"You're right," Harry said, but the look on his face said something quite different. He put the stone in his shirt pocket and went back to address his ball from the trap.

On the seventh hole, Harry was in a trap again, and again he walked to the far edge and picked something up.

"Another one?" I shouted over to him. I was chipping from farther away.

"Yeah," he said. "I don't get it. I don't get it at all." He put this one in his shirt pocket, as well.

When we finished the ninth hole, Harry said he'd like to break for lunch before going on to the back nine. I suspected he had something special in mind, probably related to whatever he had found in the traps.

We entered the clubhouse and were heading to the bar for a sandwich and a drink when we bumped into Gerry, another pal from our college days. Harry pulled him aside and began whispering to him. I walked away, but Harry called to me. "Stay here, Nick. I want to find out about the 'you know what.'"

Harry told Gerry about the "diamonds." Gerry said he didn't know anything about such things. But then

Gerry remembered that he had read an article in an old *Time* magazine in the clubhouse lounge about diamonds being found on the surface of the earth in certain parts of the United States. I brushed off the idea as preposterous, but I could see that Harry was intrigued. "You mean it's possible that a field of diamonds could be found anywhere around here?"

"That's what I understand," Gerry said. "But they must be extremely rare."

"And expensive?" asked Harry.

"I would think so," said Gerry.

Harry rubbed his eyes and then pulled his cell phone from his pocket. I overheard him say, "Come here for them in the bird, and find an expert, fast."

"What's all that about?" I asked.

"I've got to find out about these things."

At that moment, Dale walked by. Harry touched him on the shoulder. "Hey, Dale," he said, "has anyone been finding shiny things on the course?"

"Don't know what you're talking about," said Dale. "What shiny things?"

"I guess it's nothing," said Harry.

Harry wanted to go and finish the back nine, so we returned to the course. I knew it wasn't my place to give Harry any advice and certainly no criticism, unless he asked for it. But I couldn't help myself.

"Go easy here, Harry," I said. "Something funny's going on."

"Your trouble is that you never take risks. You see danger everywhere. You're paranoid, and you can't make money being paranoid. Sometimes you've got to leap into the dark."

"All right, Harry," I said. "I won't say any more."

We were in the middle of the fifteenth fairway when we heard the chopper coming. It hovered over the treetops and lighted next to the green. I was sure Dale would have something to say about that. Harry ran under the spinning blade and took the stones out of his shirt pockets and handed them to a young man dressed in a blue suit, with a blue tie and white shirt. Then the helicopter rose quickly and banked away.

"He's going to check them out and call me," said Harry. "We should know by the end of the game."

"Impressive," I said.

Sure enough, we were on the eighteenth tee when the call came in. Harry spoke softly and briefly.

He clicked his phone shut. He was looking at me, but not really, his mind already racing. "They're diamonds," he said flatly. "The best raw diamonds this expert had ever seen. The kind found on the surface of the ground rather than in mines. Worth a fortune in any quantity."

I wanted to warn Harry, but I knew he didn't want me to. He wouldn't listen anyway. His eyes told the story: they were half glazed over by this point. I saw true greed in his expression, and I thought that only something bad could come from such an expression.

"What are you going to do?" I asked him.

"Do you know if Dale owns this course outright? Any partners? Liens? Invisible investors?"

"I don't know anything about that," I said honestly. "But Harry, be careful."

"Don't mother hen me," Harry said with an odd sharpness I had never heard in his voice.

"All I know," I said, "is that the course is looking a little shabby this year. I don't know what that means, but the clubhouse is also not as clean as I remember it, and the food is a step down from the usual standards."

"Interesting," said Harry. "Good. Any other impressions or information?"

"I've heard that Dale is pretty shrewd."

"Irrelevant," Harry said.

"I think of him as a kind of Gatsby."

"Don't know him," Harry said.

The rest of Harry's game was sloppy and by the time we finished the course I was just a few strokes behind him. It seemed not to bother him in the least. We returned to the clubhouse, where Harry asked to see Dale. I was surprised at how quickly Dale appeared.

"What is it Harry?" Dale asked. "I'm a little busy. We have a function here today. Busy place."

I glanced around. I didn't notice any signs of busyness.

"How old are you, Dale, if you don't mind me asking?"

"Not at all, I'm seventy-two."

"I suppose you'll want to retire soon."

"I hope I never really retire, but yes, I guess I'll be getting out of this business one of these days."

"How much is your place worth?" Harry asked. "If you don't mind."

"I haven't thought about it. I guess ten million."

"Pretty steep," said Harry.

Dale shook his head. "Not really. Look at any golf course. They're all big investments. This place is well established, with a good clientele, a long history. It'll go on for another century. We do events as well as golf. Popular place. These days, I'd say ten million's a steal."

"Would you take eight for it?" Harry asked with a bluntness that made my knees rubbery.

"Is that an offer?"

"Yes, contingent on my doing a little research."

The air around us suddenly felt charged, electric. My heart was pounding. Harry and Dale fairly bristled with the energy of the deal, both of them with oddly predatory smiles on their faces. I could almost sense the greed spilling out of the two men.

"I'd like to check with my manager about that offer," Dale said.

"And I need a little information about the course," said Harry.

They parted with a plan to meet in two hours. Obviously, Harry didn't want the deal to linger, and, surprisingly to me, Dale didn't seem worried about the hurry. It was as though he was expecting the offer.

Harry got on his phone once again and asked for a quick study of the country club, whatever was needed as prelude to purchasing the place. Harry told his underling to expedite the whole thing. Time would be crucial.

"What do you think about this, Nick?" he asked. We'd settled into the far corner of the bar. Harry was drinking a glass of orange juice. I'd ordered something stronger.

"I don't like the looks of it. What are you thinking? Those diamonds?"

"I read the magazine article. This place could be crawling with the things, if they're showing up in the traps."

"'Could be' isn't worth eight million."

"What you don't know, Nick, is that I deal in millions of dollars every day. I never have time to get really sure of the venture I'm about to make. Sometimes they work out; often they don't. The averages work in my favor."

"In that case," I said, "I'll be interested to watch what develops."

Harry just smiled, and I saw how he thrived in the atmosphere of an edgy risk.

By four o'clock he and Dale and their subordinates and lawyers were meeting in the club boardroom finalizing the sale. They came out smiling and chatting, the lawyers going off in their limos and the others comparing their notes. Harry and Dale came over to the bar where I was waiting and wondering.

"I'd like you to meet the new owner of the country club," said Dale, obviously happy with the turn of events.

"You seem pleased," I said to him.

He shrugged. "I never thought when I got up this morning that I'd be out of a job before the end of the day. I'll just think of it as early retirement." It seemed to me that Dale was perfectly happy with the new development in his life.

Harry asked the bartender to give us all a round of drinks and we toasted him. I was sincere when I wished him the best of luck, because something in me said that he had just been taken.

Two weeks later I went to the club to play a game by myself and to see if there had been any changes in the place since Harry had taken over. Everything looked eerily the same. There was no sign of new ownership and certainly no indication of any improvements. I went to the bar to see if Joey was still around. Sure enough, he was in his usual place, cleaning glasses and wiping the counter.

"Joey," I said, sitting on the same stool I had occupied when the great meeting had broken up two weeks previously. "What's going on?"

"Off the record," he said quietly.

I patted my chest. "It all stays here."

"Okay," he said. "The magazine was a plant, of course. It gave some credence to the wild idea that there might be diamonds scattered all over the place. They were scattered, all right. By yours truly. Two or three in carefully selected traps."

"Where did you get them?"

"On loan from some of Dale's friends. He knows all kinds of people."

"Why?"

"There's a new highway going to split this place in two. There won't be a course in two years. The state's got the court's approval for eminent domain. There's no choice but to close down the place. Essentially it's worth nothing."

"Not eight million bucks," I said.

Joey choked on a laugh. "You kidding? A guy would have to be out of his mind to fall for this thing about diamonds everywhere. Your friend is missing a few clubs in his bag."

"No," I said. "It's something different."

Joey shrugged. "It doesn't matter that I told you all this. Your friend found out yesterday."

I left Joey shaking his head and smiling. Apparently he wasn't worried about his job. Then a week later I bumped into Harry in front of an elevator in an office building downtown. "How you doing, Harry?" I asked.

He motioned for me to get in the elevator and join him. We got off at the penthouse where there was a lounge and restaurant with a view of the city. We sat in plush seats in a corner. A waitress in a short glittery dress brought us drinks.

"So much for honesty," said Harry, saluting me with his glass. "How could I have fallen for that?" He laughed and seemed more relaxed than the last time I had seen him.

"You lost eight million?" I asked.

"Ten, with all the footnotes. It's the price of doing business." Harry leaned over toward me. "Nick," he said, "I hope you learned something from all this."

"I'll certainly ask a lot of questions if I ever have to consider a deal like that, and I'll know there are no free diamonds lying on the ground."

"Oh, no," Harry said earnestly. "I want you to know that you always go for the big payoff. So you lose a few times. Get taken. No big deal. Brush it off. Keep your eyes open for the next opportunity. One day the fireworks will go off."

I was stunned and appalled. And if I am to be absolutely honest, also oddly envious of Harry's philosophy and his tremendous appetite for risk.

"Let's play golf next week over at the new club they've opened up on the lake," he said with a sly smile. "Maybe there'll be gold in the water hazards."

CHAPTER 7

The Guru of Golf

David Shaw tried to sit still in the soft leather sofa in the reception area of the Golden Eagles Country Club, but he was too nervous. He had never met a guru before, and he was feeling sorry for getting himself into the situation of having to meet one now. His life was a mess. He hated his job and his wife was talking about divorce. She wanted children, but he never felt settled enough in the marriage to imagine having a family. He had begun to drink more than was his custom and he was being sneaky about it.

David was raised a Catholic and thought he'd be a Catholic for the rest of his life. His wife was a spiritual person, but, as she put it, not religious, and without her support and companionship his churchgoing came to an end.

Three weeks ago Charlotte had asked him—pleaded with him, really—to see a guru she admired and who, she thought, could help them.

"Why don't we both go?" he had asked.

"Because you're the one who is living the fully secularized life and neglecting your spirituality," she said. "I'm doing all right, at least on that score."

He had called the number his wife had given him and was told that he could have an appointment after he had filled out a questionnaire and been formally accepted for the session. Apparently the guru was a popular man and had a busy schedule of saving lives. The questionnaire asked about his activities, especially the ones that he engaged in with passion. The only passion David was aware of these days was his one for golf. He didn't play all that well, but he felt he could play seven days a week and never tire of the game. Maybe it was the relaxation he felt on the course, probably not the exercise, and certainly not the social life. Anyway, he listed golf as his passion and figured, what the hell, if the guru was worth seeing he wouldn't let a little game like golf get in the way.

The attendant at the desk, dressed in a natty outfit of black trousers, red plaid vest, and Victorian stiff high white collar came over to David and asked who he was waiting for.

"You won't believe this," said David, "but I'm waiting for a guru."

The attendant didn't blink an eye. "Oh, Guru Sakyamuni should be along any time."

"You know him?" David asked.

"Sure, he's a regular. Sort of."

"What do you mean, sort of?"

"Well, he's not your typical golfer. You'll see."

At that, David saw a pink stretch limo driving up to the entrance to the country club. It was moving slowly and truly stretching its way around the circle—it was very, very long.

A large man with a Fu Manchu moustache and bald head, wearing a black suit and chauffeur's cap, got out on the driver's side and walked around to the back of the car to open the door. Out stepped a very small man who looked a lot like Gandhi but was considerably heavier. The chauffeur opened the trunk, which could have held a small oceangoing craft, and took out a slim, tattered golf bag. He carried it like a paper bag into the clubhouse behind the guru.

"Here comes Guru G. now," the attendant said to David.

"Guru G. I thought his name was Sakyamuni."

"Did I say that? Everyone calls him Guru G."

Guru G. was wearing navy blue gym pants made out of a shiny, silky material, an oversized gray sweatshirt, and sandals. He also had a plum-colored turban on his head with a sparkling blue jewel in the center. He had various gold chains around his neck and large rings on most of his fingers. Even from a distance David could see that the guru was quite comfortable with himself and appeared completely at ease in his odd garb and in the unusual surroundings.

Guru G. smiled broadly when he saw David and immediately walked up to him and clasped two hands on David's right hand. "You must be David. I'm happy to meet you."

David had no doubt that the guru was telling the truth; he had never seen such congruence in a person—words and feelings in perfect rapport.

"Would you care to have a drink or something to eat before we play our game?" the guru asked with utter charm and straightforwardness.

"If you would," David answered.

"No, no," the guru said. "I had my meal for the day, but I wouldn't mind a glass of water."

The chauffeur went away for the water and quickly brought it back.

"Do you play well?" the guru asked David.

"No, but I love the game."

Guru G. looked relieved. He took a well-worn club out of his bag and handed it to David. "This is one of my favorites," he said. "I play only tolerably well, but I enjoy the thick grass and the sand and especially the water hazards. They can be so beautiful. And the greens so soft and brilliant in color."

"Do you often counsel people on the golf course?" David had been wanting to ask this question to ease his anxiety.

"Let's not talk shop. I think we should get right to it and go to the first tee. Shall we?"

Guru G. led the way, followed by Ganges, his chauffeur and apparently his caddy, and finally David. When they got to the tee, Guru G. asked if he could say a prayer to the spirits of nature and of play. David welcomed him to do anything he wanted. Immediately the guru sat between the blue blocks that marked the most challenging driving area and seemed to disappear in the sheer calm that had come over his body. He sat there for a full 15 minutes, not stiff and certainly not restless, but full of peace and comfort.

At the end of his prayer, Guru G. stood and scanned the area around the tee. "You first, David," he said with such authority that David stood up to the tee immediately. He felt self-conscious in the spotlight, so he teed up his ball and slowly took his practice swings. He was about to hit the ball, when Guru G., who was standing nearby, said, "David, may I offer a suggestion?"

David stepped back from the ball. "Of course."

"Think only of the ball. Look only at the ball. Forget about your swing. Do not swing properly, just swing. Think of your eyes as only concerned with the ball, as though they were inside the ball. Forget everything else."

"I'll try," said David.

"No, don't try. Just do it," Guru G. said.

David pictured himself smiling from the ball and hit it with unusual ferocity but also some grace. The ball took off from the tee, skimming the treetops that lined the fairway, and then soared into the air. David had always wanted to hit like that.

"Excellent," said Guru G. "Our lessons have begun."

Now, the guru stood up to the tee. David watched and was surprised to see his swing reach far back on his head, as if for a full, powerful attack. Instead, the club made a modest, easy circle to the ball and hit it a short distance straight ahead.

"Is this how you want me to hit the ball?" David asked.

"No, not at all," said Guru G. "This is how I hit the ball on this hole in this game today. The ball wanted to go only that far. I don't know how I can have a good score in this way, but I obeyed my body, and this is what happened." He laughed, and then grew quite serious. "David, above all, don't do what I do. You swing the way you swing, not the way I do. In everything, be yourself. Do it in the way that you are at that moment. Regardless of consequences." He shifted his attention to his ball, shaking his head. "I would like to have a good score, but I have no idea now how to get one now. I'm standing on the edge without any control over the future and without any hope." This statement seemed to delight him and he reached over to David and squeezed his shoulder as if to include him in his moment of giddiness.

Guru G. got ready for the second shot. He took an iron from Ganges, who was still wearing his dark suit. The guru stood over the ball. He looked ahead toward the green. Then he focused on the ball. His swing was smooth and quite vertical. Aggressive, you might say, except that it was miraculously relaxed. David heard the club hit the ball with a hollow sound, and the ball flew into the air and traveled 200 yards to land on the edge of the wide green.

David was astonished. "Great shot," he yelled. The guru pressed his hands together and bowed. Then he walked on toward the green.

David forgot about Guru G.'s lesson on the tee and kept his eye on the green as he smashed his iron into the ball and buzzed it off in the wrong direction. Three strokes later he was on the green with the guru.

Guru G. did not use a practice swing but stepped right up to the ball and putted about 25 feet into the hole for a birdie. David missed his first putt but got the second one in. He was already four strokes behind Guru G.

When they reached the second tee, David delicately asked the guru if they were going to do anything more than play golf. Was Guru G. here to help David with his game or straighten out his marriage?

"Whatever improves your game will also improve your marriage," said the guru. "So what do we do? Counsel your marriage or give you some golf tips? If it's all the same, I would prefer, while we are on the golf course, just to play golf. If we play well, the marriage will go well. If we play badly, well . . ."

David had no idea if he agreed with what seemed on the surface to be a preposterous notion. "So there will be no counseling. Only golf lessons."

"David, your question does not come from a good place. You are dividing your life into pieces. Think of your life as a groundhog, the one that lives near the fifth hole. Tear it into pieces and it dies. Keep your life together, like a soft animal. Learn to play golf and you will learn to be married."

"But Guru G., good golfers don't always have good marriages."

Guru G. bowed to him and smiled. "You have a point there, David, but not a terribly good one. To win at golf is not necessarily to be a good golfer."

David was flummoxed, so Guru G. elaborated. "If I win or lose, it is in the hands of God. But if I play well, it is my doing."

Guru G. went first off the tee and hit his ball, as before, a short distance straight ahead. David decided to go for the smooth swing, but he wanted to put some power into it to shave some points off his score. He took some strong practice swings.

"David—David," said Guru G. "May I interrupt once again? You are swinging too hard. Few things in life require such effort. In fact, I can't think of any that do. May I suggest that you aim for ten feet in front of you? No more."

"But I'm already four points behind you."

"Ah, do you think that way about your wife? Do you count points?"

David didn't know what to say.

"If you are behind, even in life, the thing to do is relax. Stop trying so hard. Let the ball go where it wants."

David felt embarrassed to imitate the guru, but he made some gentle and smooth practice swings. Then he hit the ball. He heard a hollow sound. The ball took off from the tee and disappeared in the air.

"Excellent," said Guru G, "I think you made the green."

"I don't know what happened," David said, as he walked with Guru G. and Ganges to the green. "I thought the ball would go ten feet."

"Then you have learned something. Sometimes little effort results in big gain. Keep your goals small and possible. Take small, steady steps."

"Forgive me, Guru G., but these are clichés. You sound like Ben Franklin."

"A good and talented gentleman. You think you are above clichés? I am not. If I can come up with a good, well-used phrase, I am happy. I have no need to be original with my material, only with my life."

Guru G. hit his second ball and it went no farther than the first one. Then he hit it again. He was now at three strokes and not quite on the green. Ganges lifted a massive driver from the bag and handed it to the guru. Without a practice stroke, he hit the ball lightly and it looped onto the green and hopped into the hole.

"You had a reason for using the driver for a small chip," David said.

"Tiger Woods does it sometimes. If he does it—he is a true guru of golf—I can do it. Some problems require unexpected means. Some people with trouble in their marriages get divorced, a strong solution, and then they discover they want to be married to that person after all. I'd call divorce a long-drive solution. I use the big club only when I am desperate."

They came to a long hole with a water hazard in the middle and sand traps lined up in front of the green.

"I have a special technique for this hole, David," Guru G. said. "I'm sure you have hazards in your marriage."

Guru G. took the large driver from his bag and handed it to Ganges, who stood up to the tee and hit the ball with a smooth but mighty blast. The ball sailed easily over the water and the traps and ended a foot from the green.

"Is that legal?" David asked.

Guru G. shrugged. "My number one rule for every occasion is this: never take a challenge on its own terms. Make it your own. Whenever necessary, abide by your own rules. Baseball invented the designated hitter. Why can't I?" He walked serenely toward the green, looking forward to his putt.

By the ninth hole, David's mind was spinning with Guru G.'s baffling philosophy. He doubted he could ever live by it; so what was he doing wasting his time learning it?

As if reading his mind, Guru G. said, "Perhaps you are thinking that I am old and foreign and different and there's no way you would want to learn my approach to life."

"Not at all," David fudged. "It's interesting, but I still don't see its relevance. Besides, I came here for counsel, not for golf lessons."

"Ah, you are obsessed with this expectation." Guru G. signaled for Ganges. The big man swiftly walked right up to David, who immediately backed away. Ganges walked him face-to-face down the slope and toward a small pond. David was tripping backward and fell without much grace into the water.

"Why?' he spluttered as he emerged, his clothes soaked and his hair dripping. "Why did you do that?"

"Baptism! You know all about that. A change of mind. You need a dramatic release from this obsession of yours. Do you understand now that golf is a spiritual path? It is like walking the labyrinth. It is a ceremony, a ritual. It makes no sense to separate counseling from the game. Let me put it simply: golf is not like life; life is like golf. Do you understand this?"

Ganges gave David a change of clothes from a duffle bag he carried with him. David went behind some bushes, dried himself with a towel, also from Ganges, and came out in a pair of tan pants and a beautiful maroon shirt that felt wonderful on his skin.

"Now we will play golf seriously," said Guru G.

David began the back nine by hitting a ball off the tee that traveled a measly 25 yards. Guru G. hit one very high that fell next to David's. He laughed heartily, and slowly a laugh came out of David. Their second shots were both long and not so high. David used his driver to hit onto the green and putted without practice swings. He wasn't trying to imitate Guru G.; it was more that he got the point of the game and knew now how to play it the way one might walk the labyrinth.

When they arrived at the eighteenth hole, Guru G. took out a pitching wedge and said solemnly to David. "Forgive me for this, but it is part of the spiritual practice." He swung with amazing grace and impossible ease, and the ball puffed out of existence, flew off the tee as though lofted into orbit.

"I think it landed on the green," David said, amazed.

"It did. I apologize. Rather embarrassing," said Guru G.

David hit well, but it took him three strokes to get to the green. When they arrived, Guru G. went to the hole and pulled out his ball. He made a 400-some-yard hole in one.

"I won't ask you how you did that," David said.

"Life sometimes requires miracles, and so the game has to have its share of them. When you play the game in a certain way, over time, over a long lifetime, you may merit certain skills. One has to learn not to overvalue them, or they can destroy you. You take them in stride, but you must take them. You may now go back to your wife and play golf with her. One day you may need a *siddhi*, as we call them, a minor miracle, and, if you have been playing well, it will be available to you."

The three went back to the clubhouse, and Ganges put the guru's clubs into the cavelike trunk of the limo.

"Another embarrassment," Guru G. said, nodding toward the car, "but somehow appropriate. Learn the joys and wisdom of poverty, but don't overlook the beauty of wealth."

"When can we play again?" David asked, as Guru G. led them to the bar.

"No more golf with me," said Guru G. "You are only allowed one game with your guru. Now you may choose to be part of my family, or you may go your own way solo. In either case, please continue to play golf as I have taught you today. There is no salvation for you without it, by which I mean the full discovery of the life that came into you the day you were born."

The bartender, the one with the red plaid vest, said to Guru G., "The usual?"

"For me, yes. What would you like, David?"

David didn't know if he should have a real drink or ask for water. "A glass of red wine."

"Excellent," said Guru G. "I will have the same, with a glass of water, please. And Ganges as well."

David was once again surprised and confused.

The bartender placed a glass of wine and a glass of water in front of each of them. Ganges and Guru G. drank their water slowly. David drank his wine rather quickly. Guru G. slid his glass of wine over to David. "Why don't you have mine? I've changed my mind. I think Ganges has as well." He pushed another wine over to David.

"You keep a person off balance, don't you?"

"It's my calling," said Guru G.

CHAPTER 8

The Man Who Hit Balls High

During his childhood and teen years Tubby Gilmore had been heavy, overweight, obese—whatever word you care to use for a nice young man who carried a lot of flesh. In his early 20s he began to thin out considerably, though he was still wider in the middle than he would have preferred. Unfortunately, the name Tubby stayed with him.

He didn't have the body for basketball, and football was more violent than his sweet nature permitted, and so in college he decided to try out for the golf team. Dr. Creeley chaired the golf department with the philosophy that every student, not only the talented ones, should have a sport, not only for physical well-being but to help develop character.

The day of tryouts was the first day Tubby had ever held a club in his hand, but he was optimistic that golf could be his game. He had watched it on television and heard his father and uncles talk about their games. He knew the vocabulary and just had to develop some physical skills.

Dr. Creeley told him to stand up to a tee on the driving range and simply swing at the ball. He wanted to assess Tubby's raw talent—or lack of it. Tubby was tall, somewhere over six feet, and he looked like a golfer when he grabbed a club and positioned himself in front of the ball. But when he took a swing, the ball popped up straight into the air and came down about a hundred feet in front of him.

"We can correct that swing. Don't worry about it," Dr. Creeley said.

His confidence was not warranted, for Tubby continued to hit the balls high into the air, no matter how he adjusted his swing. Dr. Creeley noticed that as time went on the balls went farther but not lower. On the green, Tubby was a different story. His putting was superb. From all distances and angles, over ridges and down in depressions he was able either to hole out or get his ball within inches of the cup.

"We could use a putter like him," said Dr. Creeley to his assistant, Crotty.

"But the drives," Crotty lamented.

"We'll fix that. Don't worry. It would be more difficult to improve his green play, if it were the problem."

At the end of the week of trials, Dr. Creeley called Tubby into his office and told him he could be on the golf team—provisionally. They would have to correct the loft on his drives. Otherwise, he was the most promising player they had.

Tubby was elated. He had always wanted to be an athlete and a member of some team or other. He rushed back to his dorm to telephone his dad.

"I've made the golf team," he shouted into the phone.

"How could that be?" his father asked.

"I learned from watching on TV and hearing you talk about the game. It must have got into my bones."

"And you can drive the ball, without any experience?" His father was incredulous.

Tubby didn't know what to say at first. "Well, I do have some things to learn. But coach says everything will be all right."

Tubby would have preferred a more enthusiastic reception of the news from his father, but he knew he wasn't anyone's idea of a good athlete and determined to prove himself.

His mother got on the line and asked if the game was dangerous. She heard once about someone getting hit with a golf ball. "It would be a rare occurrence," Tubby assured her, "and I have great eyesight. I'll see the ball coming and duck."

In the weeks leading up to their first games, Coach Creeley tried every trick he knew to lower the arc of Tubby's drives. But nothing worked. The ball would fly off the tee at about 50 degrees and soar into the sky like a rocket launched into space. There was something exhilarating in seeing one ball after another sail up as if into orbit—this is if you weren't concerned with distance and winning tournaments.

But Dr. Creeley was getting worried. He needed every person on his team, and unfortunately Tubby couldn't just putt around the courses. There were some drives and pitches to negotiate, as well. He explained the situation to Dr. Crawford, the athletic counselor, who offered to do an assessment of the young man.

"What is your relationship with your father like?" he asked Tubby in their first session.

"He'd like me to be an athlete like he was, and still is, but he's always disappointed in me. I'm trying as hard as I can to please him," Tubby said.

Dr. Crawford took notes at a ferocious rate. Usually he had to dig for information that had any psychological relevance, and here a perfect expression of a typical emotional problem for athletes presented itself. *The mere fact that he has given voice to this dynamic with his father will surely ease this problem,* thought Dr. Crawford.

But it didn't. The balls kept popping up vertically. Even his other teammates began to feel discouraged. The coach asked Dr. Crawford to try again.

In their next session Dr. Crawford asked Tubby, "Do you ever dream of flying?"

"All the time," said the young man. "I'm always in airplanes and balloons and rockets. Sometimes I fly on my own power, with my arms flapping. Sometimes I soar like a hawk."

"Excellent," said Dr. Crawford. "I think we've got something here."

Together they explored as many metaphors of flying they could think of: ambition, idealism, the desire to escape, fear of ordinary life, not wanting to be married, a need to remain a child.

Still, the balls kept popping up.

"We're going to work the physical angle again," Coach Creeley told Dr. Crawford.

They had Tubby hit every ball off the ground without a tee. They outfitted him only with clubs that had a low angle of loft. They told him to visualize hitting the ball along the ground. They blindfolded him and had his eyesight checked. They weighted each club and tried every trick they knew to change his swing.

Eventually, the training period was over and the team went on the road. The big surprise came the fourth day out. Coach Creeley scheduled Tubby for a team and all the coaches and players showed up to see what would happen. Tubby addressed the ball in his usual graceful fashion and hit it rather hard. The ball whizzed off the tee and traveled almost 200 feet along the ground. It bounced and hopped and kept moving fairly straight until it stopped at a point at least as good as any other player's ball. Tubby went on to hit the ball on the ground to the green and then putted brilliantly. He came through with a birdie.

Coach Creeley felt flummoxed, especially as Tubby continued to hit every ball long and low, on the ground in fact. He couldn't get a ball in the air no matter how he tried. Coach Creeley telephoned Dr. Crawford for advice.

"It's not that unusual. I knew a man who spoke in a high squeaky voice all day long, but if he ever had to speak formally, in public, his voice dropped an octave."

"So," said Coach Creeley. "What can we do in this situation?"

"I don't know," said Dr. Crawford.

Tubby continued to hit on the ground. His distance and direction were good, but his style looked terrible and demoralized his team. When they got back home, Coach Creeley told Tubby he would either have to hit a normal ball or leave the team. He was sorry, but he couldn't have the whole team feel embarrassed by one player.

Tubby called his father and explained the situation. "What should I do, Dad? They want me to hit the ball in the middle. I can't do it."

"There's only one thing you can do, son. You have to play your own game. If your body wants to hit the ball high, then let it rip. If those coaches don't understand that, you shouldn't be playing for them. Besides, I've never been a middle-of-the-roader."

The next day, Tubby went to Coach Creeley and told him he would be leaving the team. He was a high ball hitter. He couldn't change that fact, and he couldn't explain it. The coach accepted Tubby's resignation. The team went on the road again, and was relieved of the embarrassment they felt with Tubby's odd drives, but they missed him. He brought a special spirit to the game. When they got back home, the coach had a message to visit one of the trustees of the university, an old man named Principal Screed.

Mr. Screed lived in an old mansion on a broad and tree-lined street a few blocks from the athletic field. A butler opened the door for Dr. Creeley. Screed came down a curving flight of stairs and directed him to his personal library, a high-ceilinged room ringed with books. They sat in two leather chairs in front of the fireplace.

"What's this I hear about Tubby Gilmore being cut from the golf team?" Screed said without preamble.

Dr. Creeley shifted in his chair uncomfortably. "He was an embarrassment to the team, especially on the road. He hits the ball either extremely high or on the ground."

"But his score was pretty good."

"His score wasn't bad, but it wasn't spectacular, either. I like Tubby. Everyone likes him. But you have to win."

"Do you know who started up your athletic program and built your athletic center?"

"You did, sir."

"Now, I don't want to be one of those controlling, interfering philanthropists, but I don't like to see an injustice done. What's wrong with a high ball?"

"It isn't good form, that's all."

"I'd appreciate it if you'd give Tubby a chance. Let him hit high. See what happens. I don't blame him not wanting to be normal and in the middle and like everyone else. That's how I made my money."

When he got back to his office in the athletic center, Dr. Creeley went right to Dr. Crawford's office. He told him about Mr. Screed's request. "What do you think about cultivating Tubby's high balls? Let's see if he can build a game out of them."

"It'll never work," proclaimed Dr. Crawford. "His habit of hitting high expresses his neurosis. You can't build a healthy and effective athlete on neurotic behavior. I'm certain about this. It's one of the most logical and reliable judgments I've ever made."

But Dr. Crawford's adamant stance only spurred on Dr. Creeley, and he decided to give Tubby a chance to play his own game. "I'm going to coach him myself," he told his staff.

Tubby and Creeley worked together three hours each day, on the course and on the driving range, especially the driving range. Creeley tried to forget everything he knew about a good swing and worked instead toward improving Tubby's own swing. He couldn't detect what it was in the swing that caused the pop-ups, but the distance improved and the direction of the balls remained good. Tubby's pitching and chipping were also high but accurate and controlled. Overall, his game improved significantly.

When the next road trip was approaching, Dr. Creeley received a call from Mr. Screed. "I've been monitoring your practices with Tubby Gilmore. Good work. I see progress."

Dr. Creeley had no idea how Mr. Screed could possibly be watching the practice sessions. He was either using electronic surveillance or not quite telling the truth.

"I have one more suggestion," Screed said in his scratchy voice. "I believe the young man's name is Arthur. I recommend that you and your staff start calling him Arthur. Let him be a man. I don't expect any magic from this change, but I think it's appropriate."

But there was magic in the change of name. The day Arthur Gilmore stepped up as a full-fledged member of the university golf team was a celebrated day in the history of local sports. Arthur hit a high ball, but it carried and got as much distance as any of his competitors or teammates got. With his controlled pitching and brilliant putting, he became the star of the team.

People came from considerable distances to behold the odd spectacle of golf balls in the air, like fireworks making their parabolas in the sky and landing in favorable conditions for a good golf score. Other golfers who saw the magical effect tried to imitate it, but no one else was able to combine a spray of lofting balls with a superb score. Arthur seemed born to the skill.

Not only did his accuracy and distance improve, the balls started flying even higher. People compared them to spray from fireboats or ceiling ribs in a cathedral. They threatened to make rain, some said. They might never return to earth, others predicted. They couldn't be recorded on television or in any video medium, because you had to be present to the full-dimensional impact of the balls leaving the tiny tee in the ground and immediately piercing the clouds. You had to imagine yourself traveling with them in an awe-inspiring arc and coming down exactly where planned. You had to enjoy the almost comic effect of short pitches and even shorter chips sailing impossibly high and then plopping down. The balls were not kind to the greens, and Arthur had to use his divot repair tool at every hole.

"I guess I was wrong," Dr. Crawford said to Dr. Creeley at an on-campus bar after a brilliant win for the team.

"I guess you were," said Creeley.

"I have to revise my theory about neurosis and athletic prowess."

"I guess you do," said Creeley, looking happy and content.

At that moment, he heard a cough. He was startled to see Mr. Screed entering the bar, followed closely by his manservant. Screed was dressed like a 19th-century gentleman, in waistcoat and stiff collar and tall hat. The latter he removed as he sat at the small table with the two doctors.

"I was told you were here, Creeley," he said. He signaled to his butler, who returned moments later with a coral blue martini.

"You have to have an adequate philosophy. If you're lucky, you'll have an excellent one. It will be expressed in several terse statements of principle that you can remember in every situation. Oscar Wilde wanted to change the Delphi dictum from 'Know yourself' to 'Be yourself.' That is one of my principles—Wilde's, that is. You have allowed Arthur to be himself and people are being inspired and, I hope, instructed by him. So, I toast you." Screed drained his martini and immediately stood up to leave.

Creeley and Crawford didn't know what to say, except for the usual thank-yous and good lucks.

"There's one thing I'd like to know," said Creeley as he watched Screed in his tall hat make his way out of the bar. "When I was coaching Arthur, I had the sense that he was intentionally making those balls go high, in spite of all my efforts to level them off. Do you think Screed ever talked to him and offered his 'philosophy'?"

"Oh, I don't think Arthur's capable of anything so subtle," said Crawford. "He's a neurotic who caught the fancy of a financier. If only we should be so lucky."

CHAPTER 9

The Golf Hotel

When Sally and Bert's children all left for college, the couple felt that their house was too big for them and they decided to downsize. They looked at all kinds of properties—condos, lakefront and oceanfront homes, bungalows, duplexes, and, with increasing desperation, even a mobile home. Their real estate agent, Cutty, was a small man with a razor-thin moustache who talked incessantly and said very little. But they trusted him to find what they needed, since many years ago he had found the house in which they had raised their children.

One day Cutty called and said he had found their dream home—but then he always said that. He picked them up in his block-long 1980s rose-colored Cadillac. Sally sat in the backseat, while Bert took on the task of looking responsive to Cutty's endless and meandering monologue. He narrated a mix of politics, gossip, and an occasional bit of real estate information into a salad that was neither Caesar nor seasonal but a wild and quixotic blend. Bert nodded, grunted, and uttered an occasional inappropriate word that didn't register on Cutty at all.

They were on a wide, multilaned street in a popular shopping district when Bert spotted a tall elderly man pulling a golf cart down the crowded sidewalk. "Pull over," he said to Cutty in an uncharacteristically sharp tone. It was the only way to put a pause in Cutty's discourse. Cutty parked tentatively at the curb and Bert got out and approached the man with the golf cart.

"Do you need a lift to the course?" Bert asked.

"No, no," the man said distractedly. "But thanks, thanks a lot."

"We have a big trunk and could fit your clubs in."

Sally watched in alarm through the rose-tinted windows. She had no idea what Bert wanted with this man, who very well could be a mental patient or even a criminal.

"How about a cup of coffee?" Bert asked.

"Sure," the man said. "I'd be much obliged."

Bert insisted Sally and Cutty leave the Cadillac and he ushered them all into a small luncheonette and into a corner booth. The old man left the golf clubs in an alcove at the door next to a child's high chair.

"So," Bert said, "it isn't often you see someone pulling a golf cart on a sidewalk in this neighborhood. Where's the nearest course?"

"About five miles, I reckon," said the old man. "Could we have that coffee?"

A waiter came and took their order, casting dagger eyes at the city golfer.

"May I ask your name?" said Bert. His confidence in what had seemed a most natural thing to do—invite a stranger for a cup of coffee—was faltering

"Sure," the man said. But he didn't tell them.

"It's a beautiful day for golf!" Sally said brightly.

"Yes, indeed," the old man said, stopping again to watch a thought in his head. "I used to play in my backyard. It's only a block or two from here . . . I think. But the neighbors called the police. Disturbing the peace, they said."

Bert nodded his head vigorously. "There's no freedom anymore. A man can't do what needs to be done."

Sally looked worried. She had never heard Bert talk like this before.

The waiter delivered the coffee and took the knife and fork away from the old man's place, leaving him just a spoon. He left the others their utensils. The old man grabbed the jar of sugar, the glass kind with the hole in the top, and poured out several tablespoons of it into his cup. Then he poured some of the coffee into the saucer and filled the cup to the brim with milk. He sipped it loudly and a small smile came onto his face.

"This is the best coffee I ever had," he said.

"I'm glad," said Bert. "Now, can we give you a lift to the course after we finish here?"

"Thanks, no. That will not be necessary," the man said politely. "I think I'll practice my drives at home today."

"But the police," said Sally.

"Oh, my aim is pretty good. Better than it was when the trouble began before."

Sally had ordered a cup of tea made with loose leaves instead of a tea bag. The old man kept looking at her cup, and when she finished drinking it, he pointed to it.

"Do you mind?" he said.

Sally didn't understand, but she said she didn't mind.

The old man took the cup, swirled it around a few times, and then stared down into it. "I used to be good at reading tea leaves. But let's see, that must have been forty-five years ago. I wonder if I still have the knack."

Cutty was watching all of this, with a keen eye.

"Go ahead," said Bert. "We have a big decision to make. We need all the help we can get." He tried not to sound as though he were humoring the old man.

The man stared into the cup, and when he stared he seemed to leave for parts unknown. His eyes glazed over. His breathing slowed. The little tic on his cheek stopped twitching.

The others watched intently and were startled when he suddenly broke the spell and put his hand out to Bert. "My name's Aloysius, by the way. Aloysius Prendergast. My friends, when they were alive, called me A.P."

"Nice to meet you, A.P.," said Bert in a friendly way. But A.P. had resumed contact with the ethers. They could all hear his slow, loud breathing.

After a full five minutes of deep contemplation, A.P. pushed the teacup back to Sally and said loudly and boisterously, "By God, you're in for a fortune! Whatever you do, go into this deal that's being offered. Don't worry about your concerns. It's a whopper. And thanks for the coffee. I'll return the favor one day, I'm sure."

The old man got up and went for his clubs and walked out of the café. Sally and Bert were so astonished they had to order pie.

"Why did you do that?" Sally asked, digging into her slice of strawberry rhubarb.

"Do what?" said Bert. He'd chosen apple.

"Stop for this man. He's a street person. Not all there. Playing golf in his backyard."

Bert looked to Cutty for help. Cutty shrugged. "I don't know why," said Bert. "I just had this impulse. I had to do it."

Satisfied, in an odd sort of way, the threesome headed back to the Cadillac and Cutty drove to the outskirts of the city, stopping at the edge of a field strewn with old tires and refrigerators and piles of beer kegs. He got out of the car, spread his arms, and said, "One day this will be a vision of paradise: green lawns, a championship golf course, a lake, fountains, and a clubhouse and spa. And you, Bert and Sally, are getting in at the beginning. You can purchase the land and a new house to be built to your specifications at a great price now. It's sure to double when construction begins."

Bert and Sally looked at each other and then at the landfill at their feet.

"How much for the land and the house?" asked Bert.

"One mil," said Cutty. He was one of those real estate agents who prefer an intimate and casual language for money.

Bert and Sally huddled out of earshot of Cutty. "We don't have that kind of money," Sally said sternly.

"A.P. said not to worry," Bert responded.

"You can't be serious, Bert," said Sally. "A.P. doesn't even know if he drinks coffee. He practices his drives in his backyard, for God's sake."

"I've heard," said Bert, "that people who seem to be mentally slow are actually gifted spiritually. He could be an angel announcing our future."

"Bert. Don't."

"Don't you see? His golf cart was a sign, a sign of this place, heaven on earth."

Bert turned back to Cutty. "We'll do it," he said. "We'll find the money someplace."

They did find the money by borrowing heavily and selling heirlooms and cashing in some stocks and CDs. The golf course was built, the lawns planted, the clubhouse completed, and Sally and Bert's new home turned out to be spectacular. Cutty led them on a tour during the final days of painting and wallpapering.

"How many bathrooms are there?" Sally asked. "I lost count."

"Seven, I think," said Cutty. "Or is it eight?"

"We asked for two," Sally said.

"And bedrooms?" asked Bert.

"Five, apparently," said Cutty.

"We expected two," said Bert. "We were downsizing."

"I don't know what happened," said Cutty. "I noticed how big the house felt and looked at the plans. All the bedrooms and bathrooms were there."

"And the office and changing room and bar? We didn't ask for these."

Regardless, Bert and Sally moved in. They were delighted; the golf course was championship in every way. Their house backed onto the fourth hole and they enjoyed a view of three long fairways and a lake filled with tall grasses and water plants and an extravagant spraying fountain.

Sally had worried that the sounds of golfers passing all day long might disturb them, but the muted conversation of a passing foursome and the delicious thunk of a ball well driven gave them a good feeling. Both took up the game and had only to walk a few yards to tee off on the first hole.

One morning they were having breakfast when Sally said, "Bert, I do like it here, but we can't keep up with the bills. Cutty has found some more fees. I don't think A.P. was right."

"Let's be patient," Bert said with a worried look on his face. "It takes a while for predictions to fully come true."

The next afternoon Bert was taking a nap in his favorite chair, in the sunroom they hadn't ordered, when he heard a knock on the window. He looked up and saw an anxious looking man in a sweater-vest, holding a five iron, and peering in at him.

"What is it?" Bert yelled into the window.

The man spoke a few muffled words and Bert let him in the back door, near the pool that they had definitely decided against.

"I hate to bother you, but I'm here in town on business and my hotel reservation fell through. I desperately need a place to stay, just for the night. Your house is so beautiful and large . . . I'd be happy to pay more than the cost of my hotel room."

"Well," said Bert, "we do have a spare room with its own bath and sauna."

The businessman, impeccably dressed, appeared the next morning in the oversized breakfast room and thanked Sally and Bert for their hospitality and told them how much he enjoyed staying with them. He wondered if there might be any chance of doing it again on his next trip and could he mention it to a few of his associates? Bert looked confused and indecisive for a moment, but then a light went on in his head and he assured the man the room was his whenever he wanted it. Just call ahead.

Within two months Bert and Sally's B and B was doing excellent business. At least one room was occupied one night each week, and guests were more than happy to pay extra for the hominess and personal comfort of the place. The owners saw their debt diminishing layer by layer at a brisk rate. By the end of their first year, they were debating where to invest their profits, having paid all their bills and finding their rooms full now every night.

"We need more rooms," said Bert. "The demand is too great. We have a lot of dissatisfied potential customers."

Cutty said he had a piece of land for sale close to the eighteenth hole. It was waiting for development, but no one had stepped forward yet. He could sell the land for one mil.

"We can't afford that much just for land," Sally warned.

But Bert was confident. He planned on finding some investors and making a big project, perhaps a hotel with a hundred rooms.

It took a year for the hotel to be built, but sooner than expected Bert and Sally went to visit their new offices in the 250-room hotel. They had the penthouse suite for their living quarters and the lushly decorated offices downstairs. They had a competent staff and plans for other similar hotels around the world.

One day, after they had been working at their business for several months, Bert's secretary told him an odd man wanted to see him. Bert went into the outer office and saw a familiar face. "A.P.," he said. "Good to see you."

"You wouldn't have a cup of coffee, would you?" A.P. said, with a slight twitch on his cheek.

Bert took him into the coffee shop of the hotel and ordered him a big mug of coffee.

"I see you're doing well," said A.P. "I'm happy for you. You took a chance. You trusted me."

"I don't know why," said Bert, "but I liked you when I first saw you walking down the street. I thought I recognized something special in you. I didn't have to make any effort to believe you."

A.P. took a sip of his coffee, winced, and poured some into the saucer. He added milk to the mug and poured in several packets of sugar. He moved close to Bert, so that Bert could see his brown teeth and the chafed skin of his face. "I'm the archangel Gabriel," he said softly, smiling. "But let's keep it our secret."

Bert saluted him with his coffee. "Would you answer a question for me? Honestly?"

A.P. nodded. "Maybe."

"Are you really an angel or . . . forgive me for being crude . . . or are you struggling with some form of mental illness? You can guess what my wife thinks."

A.P. took another sip of his milky coffee. "There's only one word there I don't understand—*or*."

Now Bert nodded. "Let's go hit some balls."

CHAPTER 10

The Golf Lesson

The sun rose with a shock of yellow-white light on this spring morning as Josh Alameda drove the long driveway leading to the Merriwether Country Club. Josh loved golf and he loved teaching, but the combination left him cold. He had been a golf instructor for 12 years and, except for the first dozen or so lessons, he had not enjoyed it. He had to do something more significant with his life. How would he feel in his dotage, telling his grandchildren that he had spent his years teaching golf? The trouble was, Josh didn't know what else to do.

He parked his car in the oval in front of the main entrance to the club and set to work opening the shop and getting two sets of clubs ready for his first lesson that, for some reason, had been scheduled shortly after daybreak. He was polishing the shank of a well-used hybrid club when he heard the throaty splutter of an approaching car. He turned to see a polished and well-maintained vehicle of another era come to a stop beside his car.

"Good morning," he yelled to the young man climbing out of the vintage vehicle.

The boy, for he couldn't have been older than 18, waved and walked toward Josh with an exaggerated spring to his pace. He reminded Josh of the young Mickey Rooney in old black-and-white films.

"You here for your first lesson in golf?"

The young man leaned against the pro shop's blue door. He was wearing a baseball cap skewed to the side of his head, not backward, and he had on a beautiful pair of camel-colored tweed knickers.

"I am," the kid said and he held out a hand out to Josh. "I'm Kincaid."

"That's it? No Jim or Jack or Neil?"

"Kincaid."

"Okay, Kincaid," Josh said. "Let's get started."

The young man started out toward the course, the grass still sparkling with dew. "Why don't you grab an iron?" Josh advised.

"Okay," said Kincaid, full of enthusiasm. "But, what's an iron? I'm new to this game."

Josh let out a rush of air from his lungs. Innocence or ignorance? Perhaps simple naiveté. It was going to be a long morning. "If you'll notice," he said patiently, "some of the clubs have a wood base and others are made entirely of iron. These last are what we call irons."

"Interesting," said Kincaid. "I guess golf is more complicated than I thought."

"A bit," Josh agreed. He picked up the bags he had prepared and headed, with Kincaid in tow, to the first tee. "Normally you would begin instruction on the driving range, but since you don't seem to know a lot about golf, I think it would be more fun, and ultimately more productive, to start on the course."

"I like that. Golf or nothing." Kincaid grasped an iron and tried putting it behind his back and stretching. "I saw this on television."

"Good," Josh said. "Try a practice swing or two."

Kincaid reached for another club and swung it with one hand like a weed trimmer.

"Try this," said Josh. He demonstrated how to hold the club with two hands and then swung it so that its head brushed the grass with a swishing sound so soft that any seasoned amateur would have envied it. Kincaid didn't know enough for envy yet.

Kincaid gripped his club with two hands. "I don't want just to be taught how to play golf. I want to become a golfer. Do you know what I mean?"

"That's a high ambition," said Josh.

Kincaid straightened his baseball cap and pulled it lower over his eyes and swung his club in the direction of the practice green.

"So this is our first hole," Josh intoned. "We call it number one. That green you're looking at is only for practice. So grab another club, whichever one you think will do the job. It's a four-fifty-eight-yard par four."

Kincaid rifled through the bags and pulled out a sand wedge.

"Now, why would you pick that club?" Josh asked.

"I like the shape. That sharp angle appeals to me. It suggests determination."

"Okay," Josh responded with his patient teacher's voice, "but do you think it can get the ball to the hole?"

"Now that's where I need some instruction," said Kincaid. "You're telling me then that these clubs affect the ball in different ways. Can I see how big the ball is?"

"But you've seen the game on TV. You know what the ball looks like." Still Josh humored the youngster.

Kincaid rolled the golf ball in the palm of his hand with delight. "Television gives you a distorted picture.

I thought the balls were about twice the size and soft, softer than a tennis ball."

Josh looked up to the sun; the thought of prayer came to his mind. "You really don't know much about golf, do you, Kincaid?"

"I tried to tell you that. I'm a beginner."

"I see that," Josh said, still blinking away the sunspots in his eyes. "So let me begin at the beginning. Golf is a game in which a player hits a small white ball toward a green, where there is a little hole dug into the ground. The object of the game is to get the ball in the hole with as few strokes as possible. Simple."

"That's helpful," said Kincaid, still holding the wedge. "I take it that this iron I selected is not the best club for hitting the ball 458 yards."

"Excellent reasoning," said Josh.

"And I take it there's some pleasure in hitting the ball in stages toward the hole in the ground. You see, I need the basics."

"Some of us find pleasure, some of us torment. But we all find meaning."

Kincaid lowered his head as if in contemplation.

Josh continued, "Indeed some of us find it so meaningful that we sacrifice our marriages and our whole lives to it."

"Did you?" Kincaid asked.

"Well, my dad wanted me to be an engineer, and I became a golf instructor. I don't think he ever forgave me."

"No, no." said Kincaid with great earnestness. "He didn't understand. Golf is important, more important than anyone realizes."

"So do you want to learn how to play golf or do you want to philosophize about it?" Josh said abruptly. Why the hell was he telling this kid his life story?

"I can't do one without the other. Action and reflection. You don't have to reflect, but I do."

"Fine," said Josh. "Now, watch me." He teed up a ball and hit it with his hybrid. It flew straight toward the green and then rolled up onto it.

"That was a good shot, wasn't it?" said Kincaid. "It must be wonderful to get on the green."

"Try it," Josh said, stepping away from the tee.

Kincaid fished around in the bag and pulled out a five iron.

"Not enough," said Josh.

"Let's see," said Kincaid, and without any hesitation or practice swing he moved his body exactly as Josh had and hit his ball high and straight and far, and it rolled onto the green and stopped, hesitant, an inch from the hole. "I like this game."

"How did you do that?" Josh asked when they reached the green. "How did you know how to hit that ball back there? You didn't have a lesson yet."

"Beginner's luck?" answered Kincaid. "I know I came here for a lesson, but what I really want is a non-lesson."

Josh looked perplexed.

"You've never had a teaching from a Zen master?" said Kincaid. "Oh, promise me you will before the month is out."

"Kincaid! This is a golf lesson. Yours. Take it or leave, please."

"I will," the youngster said enthusiastically. "I want to become a golfer. That's all. I don't need to know how to play the game."

Josh shook his head in exasperation and he took two putts to hole the ball. Kincaid made it in one.

"May I ask you another generic question?" Kincaid asked en route. "Why are they called clubs? If you club someone, you smash them. Is that what you intend to do with your clubs?"

"Maybe in the beginning, when prehistoric people played golf, they used raw dangerous clubs, and we just use the same word."

"I sense something violent in golf," said Kincaid, gazing at the deserted fairways. "This is all so peaceful, but I'm not sure yet whether to trust it."

Josh teed up a ball, took a club from one of the bags and then called the lad over. "Use this wedge and take an easy, graceful, nonviolent swing at the ball. Hold your body fairly still, except to let it swing with the club. Don't lift up your head too soon, and look toward the ball after you swing."

Kincaid stood up to the ball and did exactly as he was told. The ball floated up high and landed about 100 yards straight ahead of him.

"Good swing," Josh said, obviously surprised. "If you had used a longer iron or a wood, you'd be much farther toward the hole."

"Oh, I see," Kincaid marveled. "That's why you use so many clubs. Each one gives you a different distance."

"That's a big part of it," Josh agreed. "Now tell me, was your swing violent?"

"No."

"Does that answer your question about golf and violence?"

"People do become violent. They smash their clubs. They cuss. They throw things. They stomp off."

"And you've never played before?" Josh asked, even more suspicious.

"No," said Kincaid. "I've seen it all on television."

"Most people who don't play golf can't stand to watch it on TV."

"It's a kind of meditation. I mean it. It's slow and quiet."

Kincaid did as well on the second hole as on the first. Josh thought that there was no way it could be his first time. His posture of ignorance was surely a sham. But Josh curiously didn't feel annoyed. There was something undeniably appealing about the young man.

By the fourth hole the golf lesson had become a game and Josh the pro was in danger of losing.

After a striking putt on the eighth, Kincaid plucked his ball out of the hole and said, "You're playing par, Josh. Great. I'm two over at this point."

"How do you know how to keep score? Forty-five minutes ago you didn't even know what kind of ball is used in golf."

"You told me, Josh, about counting the strokes. That's all I've done."

"And how can you play so well? No one scores in the seventies their first time out."

"I don't care what other people do, Josh. I'm not learning how to play. You're teaching me how to be a golfer. You've inspired me, modeled for me, and shown me a few things I shouldn't do. You're doing a great job, and I'm learning well. It's all so simple."

"Right, then let's really compete from here to the eighteenth. That will be a good lesson, too."

"All right. Just like a car race. I love a good competition."

They played a passionate game right to the end. Josh drew on all he knew and dropped a few birdies. Kincaid drew on everything he didn't know and made some birdies, too.

Going up to the eighteenth tee, Josh turned to the youngster. "Kincaid, I really enjoyed this game—or lesson, whatever it is. I haven't played golf like this in years. And I don't even know who's the teacher here."

"That's the way it should be," said Kincaid. "Do you know how Socrates taught? He let the student learn and didn't teach him anything he didn't already know."

"I was in quite a pit when you arrived here this morning. Now I feel like playing on the tour."

"You should," Kincaid urged. "You have to teach your father that golf is the most important thing in the world."

Josh cast his eyes down. "My dad passed on three years ago."

"That's all right," said Kincaid. "As long as it's within ten years, you can do it."

Josh hesitated and then spoke. "You could go on tour eventually, too. You have talent, Kincaid. More than talent. And I don't know what that extra thing is."

"This is my last game, Josh. I told you I didn't want to learn how to play, and the fact is, I don't know how to play. But I was a golfer for a morning. You gave that to me."

"You mentioned something about car races. Have you done that?"

"Oh, yes. I raced until I won, until I could honestly be called a racecar driver. But now I'm retired. I have a feeling I'm going to do a lot of retiring in my life. My teacher in India calls it 'beginner's mind.' You start by knowing nothing and end up knowing a little less."

Josh went to the tee on the eighteenth and hit a solid drive straight down the fairway and long. Kincaid still preferred a shorter club. But he swung easy and the ball drifted through the air. They came to the green and Josh hit a long putt. It was sublime the way the ball curved in toward the hole and dropped in. Kincaid was 12 feet from the pin, but he picked up his ball and pocketed it. "I like to quit a game on my own terms."

"You're a hard man to figure out," said Josh. They walked back toward the pro shop.

"It's not my game," said Kincaid. "It's yours. But if you ever again think of quitting, I'd like you to give me another lesson. I'll need one about then."

Josh walked Kincaid over to his car. "This is a Hudson, right? My dad had an old green beat-up one. He only ever drove it around his parents' farm. Do you mind?"

Kincaid stepped aside and Josh used his shirtsleeve to rub just a touch of shine on the roof.

CHAPTER 11

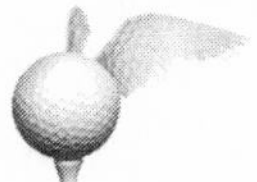

The Lost Ball

Marty Morris loved golf. He worked as a weatherman and had a passion for thunder and swiftly passing clouds, but he loved golf. With a wife he cherished and two children he adored and a job he could tolerate, he wondered how to fit golf, so demanding of time and personal resources, into his life. The answer was to play a game with three of his college buddies once a week. Eighteen holes. Canceled only when Marty determined the skies would not allow a full round.

Marty had taken a psychology course in college as an elective and he knew that there was something clinically insane about the game, or at least something insane-making about it. Non-golfers would repeat to him the tired old remark about golf being a game in which grown men chase a tiny ball. The tininess of the ball didn't bother him, but the potential in the game for making him veer toward moments of utter irrationality did. His golf buddies laughed and said that he was too much of an intellectual and should never have majored in weather.

One day in late fall Marty and his buddies played their weekly game among the piles of leaves, the low-angled sun casting long shadows. The season was coming to an end and there was a degree of desperation in their swings. They knew they were approaching the last pitch to the green, the last fairway wood, and the last long putt before winter would set in. Winter, infinitely long and nasty enough to cover the entire green course with a thick white tarpaulin of snow.

They walked somberly through brown, drying leaves that made crunching sounds beneath their cleated shoes. They brushed twigs away from balls stuck in the thick and crusty sand of traps that no longer shifted in the blowing winds. When they pushed a tee into the cold hard earth they brushed aside piles of dried grass that that offered no weighty impediment to a good swing, but only a visual illusion that they could stop the club in the full force of its arc.

They arrived at the eighteenth hole, maybe the last one in this lifetime, and they hesitated and paused and shuffled around, anything to slow down time. Marty was especially melancholic but he nevertheless stood at the tee, set the ball high for his Big Bertha driver, and swung with all his heart. It was the best ball of the season, the last and finest. It sailed into the air like a preternatural bird of prey, off after invisible game. He swore he could hear the ball hum. It soared so far and so high and straight into the setting sun that, as Marty sought its place of rest from his high perch on the tee, he was momentarily blinded.

"Where did it go?" He gasped. "Did you see it?"

"No," said his buddies. "The sun. It's too bright. Good shot, though. It's in line with the green, surely."

That "surely" tripped him up. It represented uncertainty, and if there was one thing Marty needed at this moment, it was certainty about where his beautiful lofting ball had lighted. The last ball of the season, he had used a precious, expensive celebrity of a ball given to him by the professional golfer Payne Stewart just weeks before the flamboyant golfing star had died in a plane crash.

The foursome walked off the tee toward the green in search of their tiny balls on the leafy landscape. Marty veered off to the left, where he thought his ball might have gone, if he had used his accustomed big swing and had hooked the ball. He took out his five iron and used it as a rake to clear small patches of tall yellowing weeds. Then, eyes keenly set in front of him, Marty wandered far into the forest.

His buddies called out, "Marty, come back."

But there was no way he was going to allow this final hole of a great round at the end of the season go unfinished. He sank to his knees and rummaged around the roots of bushes and the brittle stalks of summer's wildflowers.

When he finally emerged from the woods, sans ball, he looked up and down the fairway and caught no sign of his buddies. *They must have gone on,* he thought. He knew the course well and cut across a green and two fairways and caught up with them as they headed toward the clubhouse. It was their custom to have a burger and a beer before going home after a round.

His buddies chatted about the season and their scores and their advances and setbacks, but Marty didn't have the heart to join in.

"What's up with you?" one of them said, wiping a beer-foam moustache from his lips.

"I lost the damn ball," he explained. "It was a special ball, and I could have had a great score today if I had found it."

"You would probably have four putted."

"Forget it," cautioned another.

"The game isn't finished, right?" Marty said suddenly energized. "I can come back tomorrow, find the ball, and finish the last hole. Right?"

"Let it go, Marty," they all said.

That night Marty went to bed early. His wife grew concerned. He had eaten little and seemed to have something on his mind. Marty was not the depressive type. He was an ordinary guy. Heaven was an afternoon of beer and golf with his buddies.

In the middle of the night, Marty awoke in an agitated state. He remembered the day and the lost ball. Quietly he snuck out of bed and put on a pair of pants and shoes without socks. "Where are you going?" his wife whispered.

"I'm just going out for a while. I'll be back."

She looked at their bedside clock and sat up. "Marty, what's going on? It's after midnight."

"All right," he said, "I forgot something at the office. I'm going back for it. It should only take an hour."

He kissed his wife, pretended a smile, and slipped out of the house.

The drive to the course was quick and easy at that time of night. He parked a block away and entered the grounds from a side street. It could look as though he were breaking into the place if he went through the grand iron gates of the entrance.

He had brought the large flashlight he had got for his birthday and his son's battery-powered lantern as well. He set the lantern on the ground in the rough just about where he imagined the ball had gone out of bounds. He took the flashlight with him into the woods and a potato masher he had grabbed from the kitchen counter.

He was sprawled out on the ground, tearing away at the roots of a small bush, when he heard a sound familiar from many a TV program. The click of a safety being slipped off a gun.

"What's going on here?" a voice that could belong only to a policeman said.

"I'm just looking for my ball," Marty said, as though it were the most normal response one could imagine.

"Do you know that it's 3:30 A.M. and that the sun has been set for over—over—?"

"The sun set at 4:38 P.M.," said Marty with all the authority of a weatherman, "rises at—"

"Enough" said the policeman, "Get to your feet—slowly." He shone a flashlight on Marty, taking in his loosely belted pants, sockless shoes, and the torn oversized T-shirt he used for a pajama top.

"I couldn't sleep," Marty said. "I had to find my ball."

"There have been reports of a Peeping Tom in this area. You better come up with a better excuse for being here than that you're looking for a golf ball."

"I'm a weatherman," Marty explained.

The policeman motioned Marty toward the squad car with its bright blue flashing lights. He reached for his radio with his free hand.

"I've got a live one," he intoned into the microphone. "I'm coming in."

At the police station Marty was allowed a phone call, so he called his wife and told her where he was.

"I knew there was something spooky about you tonight," she said. "I'll get the lawyer over there as soon as possible. I have to stay with the kids. Marty, what have you done?"

She called his buddies and they came right over to the station. "They're trying to figure out what you intended to do with the potato masher," they told him.

"The more I try to offer a reasonable explanation for what I was doing, the worse it sounds and the deeper all the confusion becomes," Marty said. "But I thank you guys for coming out in the middle of the night for me. That's real friendship. That's what golf does to people."

The buddies looked sheepish and one of them said, "Listen, Marty, the cops were asking a lot of questions. We told them how blue you were on the course today. And then you were just so excited when you talked about coming back to finish the game. 'Manic depressive?' one of the cops asked. And we said, 'Yes, could be.' We hope you don't mind, old buddy."

He didn't. He knew what was going on; it was a classic case of leave her before she leaves you. It was much easier to minimize one's feeling for golf, to say, "Hey I don't love the game," than to deal with the grief over the approaching long and golf-free winter.

A police officer took Marty by the arm and led him into a stark, unfurnished room where his lawyer awaited. The lawyer gave Marty a close inspection from shoes to hair. "What's this about a potato masher?" he asked.

Marty told the story of what happened, and the lawyer listened without any interruption. At the end, he put his hand on Marty's shoulder and said, "All right, now tell me what really happened."

"I have just bared my soul to you," Marty confessed.

"Your buddies say that you've been acting strangely. Your wife says you tried to sneak out of your house in the middle of the night with a lie. The potato masher gave the cop who found you the willies. And you want me to believe that you were just looking for a lost ball?"

"A Payne Stewart ball," said Marty.

"This is serious, Marty. You want the police, a lawyer, a judge, and a jury to believe that you were looking for a lost ball at 3 A.M. in the dark. The game was over eight hours before. What were you going to do, play the hole through in the pitch black?"

Marty looked to the ceiling, smiled, and rhapsodized: "You hit a ball, maybe the last one of your life, and it feels like magic as it is launched by the sweet spot on the fat club. You watch it fly into the sky in the right direction in a perfect trajectory. But the sun blinds you for an instant and you lose sight of it. What do you do? Do you go home and wash the dishes?"

"And the potato masher?" the lawyer asked.

"I needed a tool to scatter the leaves. Ask any golfer. It was my rake."

"A potato masher out of context is a sinister thing," the lawyer explained.

There was a knock on the door, and one of Marty's buddies came in and tossed a little round white thing at him. Marty was shocked.

"Where did you get this?" he asked. "It's my ball. The one I was looking for."

"The group behind us found it on the edge of the green. They gave it to us, but you had left. It appears that your drive reached the green in one."

"Why didn't you tell me when you got here?"

"You were so agitated. We were worried about your state of mind."

The next morning the police captain arrived at the station and heard the story. He ordered Mary released. He was a golfer and understood. "I've used a masher on a golf course more than once," he said to his officers.

Back home Marty gathered his wife and children around the dining room table. "Everyone has to have something to make them insane," he explained to them. "You have to keep your passion alive somewhere safe, so it's available to you where you really need it. Do you understand?"

"No," his wife said. "But then, I've never studied meteorology."

CHAPTER 12

Mystic Green

Sarah Worthington was a feature writer for a midsize city newspaper in New England. She wrote the usual pieces on human-interest themes and local events complete with color photographs for the Sunday edition, but she had her eye on a much bigger calling in a much bigger city. Whenever a scandal showed itself, she would be on hand, getting all the dirty details and tracking the story mercilessly, regardless of reputations damaged and careers lost. But these darker reports were rare, and most people thought of her as a community cheerleader.

One day she was covering a local fund-raising event at the country club when she saw something that made her nose itch—metaphorically—a signal that a newsworthy item was within sight. A foursome of women had just finished up at the eighteenth hole and was walking off the green. Two of the women Sarah knew were business leaders and members of the club. One was a golf pro. The fourth was a stranger, but her face was oddly familiar, and somehow Sarah's intuition, razor sharp and seasoned, grasped an incongruity or a potential scandal in that face on that green.

Sarah had learned to trust her "gut feelings," even if they made little sense at first. She had a number of casual "informants" at the country club, including George

Fisher, a handyman who just happened to be parking some golf carts behind the clubhouse. George had been a good source for more than one story of business and political shenanigans being lived out on the golf course. The day was hot and, before approaching George, she bought a bottle of soda from the vending machine standing outside the clubhouse.

"George," she said in her friendliest manner while offering him the drink, "do you know that woman in the plum-colored shorts who just walked off the green with Marge Sutter and Mary Bonifonte?

Like most outdoor workers, George had to settle himself for a little thought before answering. He removed his cap, wiped his forehead, and scratched his head. "No."

"I've never seen her here before, but there's something about her face that's familiar," Sarah commented.

"Yuh. I've never seen her and don't have a clue who she is. I do know she's nice. She spoke with me a little before playing her round."

"Oh?" Sarah said with a little hope. "What did she talk about?"

"She doesn't play much golf but enjoys this course. The three friends like to play and occasionally make a small wager. That's what she said."

"Not much help," Sarah said softly. "If you hear anything about her, would you let me know, George? There's something about her. She's not the country-club type. I may want to do a feature on her."

"Sure thing," said George, who then went back to his job.

Before going back to her cubby at the paper, Sarah took out her tiny Leica camera and, shielded by a well-placed yew tree, snapped a picture of the attractive, mysterious woman.

Back at the paper, Sarah printed out five copies of the photograph and first asked around the building if anyone recognized the woman. No one did, but Sarah wasn't going to let it go yet. She called Marge Sutter, whom she had met during an interview with her husband, and asked if they could meet.

An hour later, Marge opened the beautifully carved and expensive door to her beautifully built and expensively fitted house and invited Sarah into a small sitting room for tea.

"Nice to see you again," Marge said, looking fully relaxed and interested.

"I'm pursuing the seed of an idea for a story," Sarah confided, "and I need a little information just to get me started. I happened to see you at the country club earlier today and I knew the people you were playing with, all except one, the woman in the plum-colored shorts."

"You mean Mary Bonifonte," Marge said, with a hint of evasion that didn't go by Sarah. "She's a good friend and an avid golfer. It's so much fun to play with her."

"No," Sarah said. "I know Mary. I mean the one in the plum-colored shorts. Not the pro."

Marge's body tensed up so slightly that only a Sarah Worthington probably would have noticed. "Yes, I just met that woman. Let me try to remember her name. Judith, I think she said. You know what it's like; you can play an entire game and then forget the name of the person you've been playing with." She laughed nervously.

"That's funny. George said you were all good friends."

Marge smoothed out her skirt and primped her hair. "I don't think George is an expert on relationships at the club."

"Can you tell me anything about the plum-shorts woman?" Sarah asked.

"No. Nothing." Marge said quickly and succinctly.

"Are you sure, Marge? I could use your help."

"Look, Sarah. I don't want to lie to you. It's just a matter of privacy. Judith wouldn't want her name in the paper." Marge's statement inflamed Sarah's curiosity and made her determined to follow up on her intuition.

Sarah stopped briefly at her office. It was around quitting time for the regular staff—reporters like Sarah worked odd hours. A young man who worked on the presses came up to her cubicle and said, "That picture you showed me. I think I know who it is."

He remembered seeing her picture in the paper not so long ago. She was so beautiful and had the same last name as one of his friends from high school: McCortle. "I think her name was Joanna," he added.

Joanna, not Judith? Sarah thanked the young man and turned to her computer to Google her. No Joanna McCortle, except for a genealogy table that offered no useful information. She tried Judith McCortle. Nothing. She had come to a dead-end for the moment, but she knew from experience that dead-ends are only temporary.

Sarah was driving home when a miracle happened. She saw the plum-shorts woman getting into a car outside a hotel. Sarah pulled to the side of the road and waited; when the woman, who was alone, drove off, Sarah followed her. Sarah tailed the shiny late-model Jaguar sedan all the way to the airport. She followed the woman into the terminal and down an escalator to the ticketing lines. She stood behind her prey for a few moments, relishing the satisfaction of having tracked her down. Then she tapped her on the shoulder.

"Excuse me—I'm a reporter for the local paper and I wonder if I could ask you a few questions about a piece I'm writing."

The woman was quite beautiful up close, perhaps a bit overly made up. She was also tall and imposing. "I'm going to San Francisco. I'm afraid I don't have time."

The line was short, and the woman would soon have her boarding pass. Sarah had to think fast. Could this story be worth a trip to San Francisco—an airline ticket, purchased minutes before the flight, a big-city hotel probably, and who knows what other expenses? There may be no story at all, but she'd had that tingling sensation in her nose—metaphorically speaking. Sarah bought a ticket.

On the plane she sat next to "Joanna" thanks to an easily manipulated airline representative at the counter. Sarah gave her time to get comfortable and then asked her, "Would you mind telling me what you do, where you're going, that sort of thing?"

The woman looked at her with a smile. She didn't appear angry or disturbed by Sarah's pushiness. "My life is private. I will talk to you about anything in the world, except myself."

Sarah found it difficult arguing with someone so self-possessed. "It's going to be a long ride."

"Why don't you tell me about yourself?"

Something in the way the woman asked the question momentarily quieted Sarah's drive. She sat back and began telling her story, thinking that it was a way to create enough intimacy to get some information. But somewhere midway through Sarah's life story, Joanna fell asleep.

At the door of the airport in San Francisco they parted. "It was nice meeting you and sharing a ride," the woman said, holding out her hand to Sarah. "I don't think we'll be seeing each other again, but good luck with your story."

When she left in a taxi, Sarah copied down the number of the cab. She couldn't risk following her closely, now that they knew each other by sight. But through a little cajoling, whimpering, demanding, and tears while talking to taxi dispatch, she was able to discover the woman's destination.

The next morning she rented a car and drove out to the Pacific shore in Marin County. She parked behind a grove of eucalyptus trees and got out of the car with a pair of high-powered binoculars. She had brought sandwiches and drinks and was ready for a long, patient wait.

Within ten minutes Joanna appeared alone on a high redwood deck, looking out on the sparkling ocean. She was wearing a turban or something like it, with a jewel in the center. The stone glistened in the sunlight. She began a series of yoga positions and seemed to be chanting or praying. Sarah had tried yoga and was immensely impressed with the woman's form, the bowlike arch of her back, the enviable erectness and length of time she remained in the Tree, a posture that Sarah had never been able to master.

The woman settled into a half lotus and when she hadn't moved in what seemed like hours, Sarah began to scan the coastline. Sea birds were plunging into the ocean close to shore and she spent quite some time mistaking a piece of kelp for a sea otter. She took a sandwich break; the woman still had not moved. She watched several more hours, off and on, until the sun set over the sea. Then she saw Joanna walk into the darkening house. Sarah expected lights to come on, but the house remained dark and still. It appeared that she had gone to bed.

Sarah decided to return early the next morning to see if she could find a lookout spot that was closer but just as safe. But when she arrived at the eucalyptus grove she saw that the woman was already meditating. At about ten in the morning, after several hours of yoga, she took an outdoor shower, dressed, and got in her car. Sarah followed.

This time she was driving a small Fiat and Sarah followed her to a rundown neighborhood in San Francisco's inner city. Dressed in white leggings, white tunic, and a head scarf, the woman spent a half hour in what appeared to be a health clinic. Then she came out with two other people, carrying baskets and boxes of food and clothing. The three walked a block and began handing out the food and clothes to people who appeared from side streets and alleyways. Several of the people bowed to her.

After three hours of work on the streets, during which time the woman returned several times to the clinic for supplies, one of the men working with her walked toward Sarah. She ducked even lower down in her seat but he knocked on the passenger window.

"Sister Joanna would like to speak with you now, if you are free."

Sarah's heart pounded. She approached the small crowd on the dismal street and saw people stroking the woman—Sister Joanna—as if to receive power from her.

"Welcome to my world," Joanna said with a smile. "Why don't you spend some time with me this afternoon?"

"What's going on here?" Sarah asked. She was confused, maybe for the first time in her life.

"I'd like you to help me distribute some food this afternoon in a project near here. Then I wish you'd come back to Marin with me and I'll tell you then what's 'going on.'"

Sarah felt she had no choice. She went door to door with Joanna in a poorly maintained high-rise project in the same neighborhood, delivering food and medical supplies. The poverty that Sarah saw that day stunned her, as did Joanna's grace and the easy way with which she laughed with some of the building's residents or prayed with others. She seemed to know most people by name.

On the way back to Marin, crossing the Golden Gate Bridge, Joanna took off her head scarf and shook loose her long red hair. The incongruity of the moment—she looked like a supermodel, enjoying the freedom of the road—jolted Sarah's memory.

"I remember what I read about you. It was in our paper. An article about how you're another Mother Teresa, giving her life to the poor." She shook her head. "And what I see is that you're a total sham, someone who play-acts at being a do-gooder and lives a secret life of luxury. No wonder your East Coast friends are lying for you."

"You're hissing," said Joanna. "Lighten up, Sarah. The world isn't so corrupt."

"Then help me understand you."

"I do yoga at a friend's house on the beach, drive a car that belongs to the woman who supports our work in the city, deliver much-needed food and medicine five days a week, and play golf to relax." Joanna spoke with her usual calm.

Sarah pulled the small Leica from her bag and snapped a photo of Joanna. "You certainly don't look like Mother Teresa at this moment." They were nearing Sausalito and the highway's turn toward the ocean.

"I never said I was Mother Teresa. People think in broad categories. They hear I'm delivering food to the poor and so they draw a conclusion. Thousands of people, men and women, old and young, are working in soup kitchens and food programs all over the country. In a way, we all have a tiny bit of Mother Teresa in us. But we're individuals, too. Personally, I am trying to blend poverty and luxury in my life. That concept may be new to you, but it's fascinating to me."

"So you don't see any contradiction in meditating for hours, working in a poverty food program, and playing golf at the country club?"

"None." Joanna pulled the car over at a parking area overlooking the ocean and switched off the engine. "I don't like telling my story, but you give me no choice. I'm a Benedictine nun, Sarah. I live in a community where I get support for my lifestyle. Most of the nuns agree with me in their own way. We own everything in common, but some of us think that to be truly spiritual you have to enjoy life fully, including, in moderation, its luxuries. We don't overdo it. I like golf. I love golf, in fact, and in some mysterious way I see it as part of my spiritual practice. It complements my yoga and my community work. I don't play often, but I enjoy it when I do."

Joanna's calm demeanor and the fact that she spoke with no hint of defensiveness left Sarah feeling off balance. Everything about the woman confounded her.

"I haven't seen any Benedictine community."

"Times have changed. Today some nuns choose to live part-time in a big community and part-time with just a few. We're individuals coming together when it feels right. The life is complicated and not always easy, but overall it's wonderful."

"What about love?" Sarah probed. She had had enough pain and complexity in that area to make her a workaholic.

"If I met someone this afternoon I wanted to marry, I'd probably do it and leave the community," Joanna said.

"You haven't made a commitment?"

"Not in the old sense. I commit myself every minute, but I leave the future open. I don't feel obligated. I want this life, and if there ever comes a time I don't want it, I'll leave. My life is a constant choice. I feel free."

"You want me to write all these things?"

"No, I don't. I'd like you to understand them and find it in yourself to accept me for who I am."

Joanna drove to the beach house. The two women got out of the car and took in the restless ocean heaving its infinite blue before them. The cries of sea birds were raucous; the wind, gusting off the headland, whisked their words away. They had to almost shout at each other to be heard.

"Stay with me a while. I have the house for the rest of the week. I do a lot of meditating and praying. You might enjoy the break."

"I guess I can spare a couple more hours." Sarah asked.

"No, let's swim first. There aren't many days you can go in the water here. Do relax, though. Try just being with me for a few hours without all the judgments."

But Sarah's deep distrust of human nature wouldn't disappear quickly. Sarah went to the car, ostensibly for clothes, took out her cell phone, and dialed the archbishop's office. She told the priest who answered that she was a reporter fact-checking an article and wanted to know if Joanna McCortle was a nun in good standing.

"I don't have to look that up. Joanna's a Benedictine. Is there a problem?"

"If she's a Benedictine," Sarah said, "I'm the pope's confessor. She's living it up with some guy at a house on Stinson Beach."

"You must be mistaken," the priest said. "But we'll look into it."

The two women swam for a half hour and then sunned themselves on the sliver of beach below the house. It made no sense to Sarah how a person could be both a mystic and a pleasure seeker. How could the beautiful lithe woman lying next to her—in a bikini—be a nun? She closed her eyes, convincing herself that she'd done the right thing in calling the archbishop's office.

Joanna was chopping vegetables when the doorbell rang and two men dressed in casual clothes came in.

"Hi, Joanna," said the tall thin one.

"Hi, Timmy," she answered. "This is my new friend, Sarah. She has some concerns about my lifestyle."

"So I hear," said Tim. "This is Greg. He's from the chancery. I thought I'd bring him along to make an official investigation."

"Good idea," said Joanna.

Greg was more serious and formal.

"Ms. Worthington," he said stiffly, "we don't want any misinformation getting out about our nuns. Have you had a problem here?"

They all sat on a sectional sofa in the large high-ceilinged room. Joanna presented vegetables and juice in large earthen bowls and jugs.

"I take my job seriously," Sarah said. "My readers deserve to know when a public figure presents herself to the world in one way, yet in private lives with a different set of morals. Here we have a nun, apparently, who has a reputation for self-sacrifice and I find her playing golf at the country club, driving an expensive car, enjoying a beach house, jetting across the country."

Joanna didn't say anything, but she looked pained.

"None of this belongs to Joanna," Father Tim said in her defense. "She works hard in the inner city, and I happen to know that she has an intense spiritual practice. Being her friend, I also know that she believes in mixing the good life with service and prayer."

Greg said, "Sister Joanna works long hours in the projects, Ms. Worthington, and besides, I play golf, too."

"So the two of you don't think there is anything wrong with this picture?"

The priests sat and said nothing.

"Sarah," Joanna said, "I don't want to defend myself. But I'll tell you this much: I fly between the coasts because my abbess asks me to. I am obeying orders. I'd rather stay in the city. And I see how difficult it is for you to understand this, but I believe strongly that God is to be found in the good life as well as on the streets of poverty. You'll definitely find him—or her," Joanna said with a smile, "on the golf course."

The men left and Joanna prepared a small meal. She asked Sarah to sit with her quietly for an hour, and afterward she placed her hands on Sarah's head in blessing. During the night Sarah dreamed of a flood, and in the morning Joanna took her to the airport. She was silent in the car for a long while, and then she said, "I get it."

A few weeks later, Sarah arrived at the country club with a golf bag and a set of clubs. A photographer from the paper was there and he gestured to Joanna, who was just leaving the clubhouse and walking toward the first tee. "Isn't that the woman you were going to write about? All her secrets revealed?"

"She's really not all that interesting," said Sarah.

Sarah joined Joanna on the first tee, along with Marge and Mary, and they made a few quiet bets before beginning their sacred game of golf.

"I see you've gotten to know Joanna," Marge said to Sarah, as the two ambled off in the direction of their golf balls.

"Yes, I know now why you protected her from me. Sometimes you have to change deep down before you can understand something."

CHAPTER 13

The Opposite of Remorse

I was just learning to play the game of golf. There were twin courses a mile from my house: one a grand country club with beautifully kept greens and fairways, always watered, always freshly planted; the other was a family course that was interesting enough with its natural hazards and hills and trees, but it was left patchy and dry and in ill repair. I chose the second. I believed that as a beginner I would be more comfortable on forgiving links, where children and duffers played regularly and where well-tailored and equipped players, skilled or not, wouldn't lower themselves to be seen.

I was somewhat diffident in those early days, not knowing the rules and etiquette of the game and unfamiliar with the informal mores of the course. Everyone seemed to know everyone else, too, and initially I felt a stranger. No doubt this was due more to my own shy personality than to any failure of hospitality of the staff and members.

And so I welcomed the warm attention of a man in his 60s who drove about speedily on an electric cart, taking care of affairs and concerns I knew nothing about.

Every time I played, or tried to play, he would buzz by once or twice, call me by name, and ask about the weather. He was a chatty man, just what I needed to get over my reticence in the golf culture.

I also became friendly with the man at the till who gave me a tee time and collected the fees. Mike was his name and he loved to gossip and tell jokes. He seemed to know the name of every member who came to play and many of the visitors, as well. I envied Mike's and Joe's—the man on the electric cart—casual ways and ease with people. I never saw them together but I would see each of them every time I played a round.

According to the gossip that leaped from hole to hole on the course, Mike was an excellent player, but the length of his drives was diminishing as he grew older, and he could be gruff and uncongenial as a partner. Once I learned of his skill, I took to asking him for tips every time I paid my fee. He was generous with his help, but one day he told me to ask Joe about a subtle matter of technique.

"Joe, you know, could have been the best golfer in the world. He was a genius, a natural talent."

I was surprised to hear this about Joe, since I had never seen him with a club in his hand or heard him say much about golf. He was always laughing and talking about the weather. Even when he complained about the way people littered the grounds, it was in a generous and forgiving manner. As I picture him in my memory, he is sitting in his electric cart with a smile on his face ready to speed off to do some other chore. In my memory I can't get a golf club in his hands. Not until the singular moment that is the subject of my little dissertation here.

One day, after Mike let it be known that Joe knew a thing or two about golf, I asked Joe about his experience of the game. He suddenly looked uncomfortable and uneasy. "I don't like to talk about it," he said. "I don't know why, but the old golfing days are on the other side of a bridge in my life, and I don't want to cross back over it."

"That's all right, Joe," I said. "I don't mean to pry."

"Thanks," he said to me. He gave me that broad generous smile, and then added, "I like you. You're not pushy. You keep to yourself and seem serious about your game. So, I don't mind telling you a little of my story."

Joe was sitting in his golf cart with one leg up on the seat, leaning back and looking as restful as the machine allowed. I sat on the grass next to my own pull cart.

"I come from a family of golfers," Joe began. "My dad taught golf at several universities. My mother played, too. I grew up swinging a club, and when I went to college I had a golf scholarship and did quite well on my team. I was elected the amateur most likely to be successful in this game, and I turned pro when I was twenty.

"I had a friend, a buddy, to be more accurate, at that time, who lived on the same street. Nate came from a big family, and his father was a truck driver. I loved his home and felt more comfortable there, having dinner and sometimes spending the night, than in my own home, with my traveling father and busy mother, both of whom lived for the culture of golf. The game defined their lives.

"I remember the first game I played as a pro. My mother and father were there in the crowd, but Nate wasn't there because his sister was celebrating her sixteenth birthday. He said he couldn't miss his sister's sixteenth for anything. I played that game like a bolt of lightning. Everything worked. My swing was as natural as the appearance of the moon at night. I could do no wrong. I broke the course record. I made good money. But I would rather have been with Nate at his sister's party.

"After that first game, I knew that if I continued to play golf for a living, I would never enjoy the life I had tasted in my friend's house. The sheer ordinariness of it satisfied something big and deep within me. I knew that if I became the success my friends and my parents thought I would be, I would have to sacrifice something that was a sine qua non for me—ordinariness, anonymity, and even the daily struggle to make a living. This may seem crazy to you, Gary, but it meant everything to me.

"So I never played in public again, never made a dollar at the game, never taught a single lesson, and, in recent years, rarely played. I still love the game, and I struck gold getting this job being a general fix-it man on the course. I couldn't be happier. I love seeing the sun and shadows on the greens and smelling the fresh air and watching all the creatures in the ponds and streams. I enjoy watching people play, and I take deep satisfaction in knowing that I don't have to show off my skills or deal with more money than I can handle. Does this make any sense to you?"

"Actually, it does," I said honestly. "It's best to do what you need to do. You can't live your life to satisfy someone else's needs and desires."

"As you can expect, my parents were shocked and disappointed when I ended my career. They suggested I go to a sports psychiatrist and sort myself out. I knew that the problem was that I *was* sorted out."

"You stood up to a lot of pressure."

"I did, but it was so clear to me what I needed to do, I didn't feel any remorse later. I felt the opposite of remorse, whatever that is."

For some reason, this conversation with Joe inspired me to take my game more seriously. I signed up for more lessons and played an extra round each week. I became friends with Mike and Joe and felt comfortable around the course.

One day the course across the road, the real grand country club, offered a free day of golf to members of the course on the other side of the tracks. I was surprised at the difference in atmosphere there. Their golfers were more formal about procedures and rules; they dressed much more carefully and expensively. They played better, though many still shanked their golf balls and lost balls in woods and ravines. They were catty and aggressive about other golfers on the course, complaining that they were slow or fast or not encouraging playing through or two players using a single set of clubs. I longed for the simpler life of the beginner's course and understood a little of what Joe was talking about.

My first season ended and the second began. Mike and Joe were both in their places, and my game was improving a tad. One day Mike told me there was going to be a tournament, the best of each course playing against each other for a prize. The country club course, called simply "A," would play us, "Z," and the winner would get $50,000 for a fund to teach youth how to play the game. It was a strangely concocted prize, all the money coming from the same place, and seemed to cover over a rivalry someone felt between the two courses. I was never aware of any competition; it may have been coming solely from A.

After the tournament was announced, the sense of competition grew daily among members and guests alike. I could sense it developing even in me. We would show those high-class dandies that we weren't a bunch of anarchic, ungifted, empty-headed golfers who couldn't do any better than to resign ourselves to a Z existence. We would use the money to keep our ranks high in number and well trained in the game.

But then word came down to us by way of the gossip chain that they were going to use two members who had been on the pro circuit and played regularly in the 1970s. Mike checked the records in Z's poorly kept files, but couldn't come up with anyone who could come close to defeating A's retired professionals. That's when I thought of Joe.

I asked Mike if he had considered asking Joe to participate, but Mike said that he had made a pact with Joe long ago never to ask him to do any such thing. Mike knew that Joe and I had become friends, and he suggested I approach Joe with the idea. I took some time to think about the plan—I had several reasons to hesitate. I didn't know if the stories about Joe were exaggerated. It happens. Maybe he wasn't such a great golfer after all, or maybe he had lost any talent he had had. Besides, I didn't want to risk my friendship with Joe, and this odd tournament wasn't worth the cost of a friend. I also assumed that someone else must be closer to Joe: I had been around the club for only a year.

But the fever around the contest grew. Within weeks it felt as if life itself was somehow at stake, and I decided to approach Joe. We were sitting as usual in the shade of some trees, Joe in his beloved cart with his leg up and I on the grass.

"Joe," I said. "You know about this tournament coming up. Have you thought about playing in it?"

"Never," he said with the finality of death.

"It would mean a lot to the folks over here if we won that money."

"It's just a stupid competition. Put a house on each side of a road, and the people living there will make up a rivalry in no time. It isn't the money; it's the ego."

I let it go that day, but in the following days I mentioned the kids who would gain so much from learning a good sport and even the value of a little pride gained for us ordinary players who always feel looked down upon from the other side of the road. That feeling of being an ordinary second-class citizen hit a mark somewhere in Joe. I sensed him faltering.

Over the next few weeks I chipped away at Joe's resistance, and finally one day he said he would do it. I asked him if he'd like some time away from his chores to tone his game, but he declined. His game didn't need any toning.

A week before the tournament he told me in the shade of a tree that he was getting cold feet. He was sorry he had agreed to contradict some basic rules he had set for himself. But he had given his word, and he would go ahead.

On the first day of the two-day tournament, Z team started its 12-person field by quickly sinking deep on the scoreboard. Where, I thought, did we get these golfers? They had even less confidence than I had on the course. On the other hand, A team must have had more than two retired pros, because they were leading by ten strokes.

Joe was the last of our team to tee off. He stood up to the ball and swung at it with such perfect form that the small crowd gathered around him—mostly Z supporters—were stunned. Word got around, and quickly Joe picked up a cadre of devotees, as he burned up the course. Single-handedly he brought Z closer to the top of the scoring list. And he only got better as the day went on.

At the beginning of day two the teams were even, but Z pulled ahead with Joe's remarkable form and style. He looked as though he were primed for the big time, and I wondered how he could have remained in such good form when he spent most of his time sitting on an electric cart, doing odd jobs.

I was in the crowd when Joe walked off the thirteenth green after scoring another birdie. He didn't look happy. He spoke quietly to me. "Gary, I hate this. I don't like being watched. I don't like crowds of people around me. I don't like the burden of having to win. And I don't like the lust for glory in their eyes. This is the last time, Gary. I shouldn't have done it."

I could see that Joe was suffering through the tournament, even though another person might consider it the peak experience of his life. I regretted talking him into it, but I couldn't think of a way out at this point. I could see, though, that the more he achieved on the course, the more pain he felt.

I went to Mike and told him how much Joe hated what he was doing. I asked if there wasn't some way we could gracefully withdraw Joe from the event. Mike looked at me as though I had asked him if he would like me to schedule a liver operation for him.

"Do you know what this tournament means to the people who play on our second-rate course? Do you know how much good that money will do for us? So Joe's a little uncomfortable. Well, tomorrow he can go back to his dear little golf cart."

Joe played it out and ended up, as he and I expected, at the top. He won for the home team and was congratulated and thanked and celebrated for the next month. New people came to the course asking if Joe would give them lessons. Some requested only that they watch Joe play. Someone offered him money for appearances. One day I noticed that Joe's cart was no longer buzzing around the course.

"He went south. That's all I know," said Mike. "He quit early yesterday morning. He left a letter for you, Gary, and asked me to be sure you got it. He said he was sorry he didn't have time to say good-bye."

I opened the letter slowly, not wanting to read it just yet, but needing to know what happened to Joe.

"Dear Gary," it read. "Sorry to escape without saying anything to you. You've been a good friend. As a friend, you know I can't stand the hoopla around me. The thing is, I love the game, Gary. I love golf. It's my life. But I can't stand the money, the contests, and the people putting all their emotions on me. I know I'm a coward to cut and run, but I don't know what else to do. It would take years for people there to forget about me. So I'm going to a new place. I'll tell you where as soon as I find out. Come see me. You love the game, too."

Two weeks later I got a call from the manager of a golf course a thousand miles away. Joe had given him my name as a personal reference. He was applying for the job of assistant groundskeeper at a small family-style course.

"I heard some rumor about Joe being a great golfer. Is that true?" he asked me.

"I haven't heard any rumors about that," I said, shaping the truth as carefully as I could. "I do know that Joe loves a good golf cart. He'll keep the course looking great and the golfing public happy. He's great for the game of golf, but don't expect any more of him."

Two months later I went to visit Joe at his new place. He sat in his cart with his leg up and I sat on the grass. He looked relaxed and happy.

"I figure I owe you an explanation," he said. "I need to be an ordinary person, to live in an ordinary town in an ordinary house. It's probably some neurosis that someone could cure, but I'm not sure I want a cure. I don't want adulation, money, or students."

"I can appreciate that."

"I also love an ordinary Monday-morning-with-a-few-friends game of golf. It's warm here in the winter—maybe you can come down here and play. You could lease a place for a few months." He smiled. "I'm lonely, I admit it."

I looked deep into Joe's eyes, considered his rather odd invitation, and said something I hadn't thought about or intended to say.

"Okay, Joe. I'll come down. But on one condition: you start playing professional golf. I'll be your caddie and business advisor. I've been studying for a business degree, and I love the game of golf."

Joe looked shocked, as if he had been betrayed.

"Not you, too, Gary," he said.

"I think you can have both, an ordinary existence and life in the limelight. I appreciate your sensitivity to the public and money and all that, but on balance I'd like to see you make a big contribution to the world. I know you can do both. That's my offer."

"I thought you knew me, Gary. You of all people. And you're trying to get me to play, just like everyone else is. You want me for your fledgling business plans."

We parted friends, but with a wide hazard between us. I went back up north to my studies and the duffer's course.

Two weeks later I got a call from Joe.

"I thought about your offer, Gary. I'm ready. Come on down."

I still don't know what got into my head to confront Joe. I'd never thought through the issues of his life, and I never had any opinion, except to trust him. An angel must have passed by that day when I told him to get off his butt and get into life.

As a golfer, he has reached the upper echelons, and as a person he has revealed all the virtues that I saw hidden in the man on the electric cart. He uses his money well, mostly for others and not himself. He enjoys the happiness he sees in his fans and followers and doesn't seem to worry about the dark side of glory.

For my part, I'm happy to still be Joe's friend and sometimes caddie. I've learned from him to appreciate the ordinary joys of life. But I didn't truly trust him until he decided to play golf for real. Ordinary life is great, but golf is something else.

CHAPTER 14

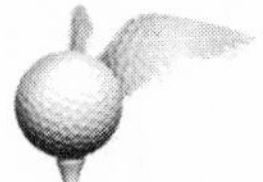

The Devil Plays a Round

Mike Connelly had an ache somewhere deep in the pit of his body. Ever since the day he saw Jack Nicklaus on television, swinging a driver, he knew what he wanted to do in life. He pictured himself walking the fairways with the greats of golf, accepting the applause of fans on the sidelines, and putting his signature on fabulous checks won on a golden Sunday on a course in paradise. How could one possibly live a more exciting life than by becoming a pro golfer and eventually a sports legend?

Mike was given to mighty ambition and stratospheric flights of fancy. But he took his flights seriously and was working hard at his game. It was a good thing that his father was wealthy and had paid for his lessons and the best and latest equipment when he was younger. If his mother had lived, she, too, would have done all she could to help him attain his ambitions, but she had passed on when he was in middle school and he felt an emptiness where her support used to be.

Mike had another equal ambition: to be a famous medical researcher, another Jonas Salk. He had struggled through medical school and residency and postgraduate studies and landed a plum position in a private research institute. He was paid well and given the freedom to pursue his dreams and follow up on any inspiration that came to him. In some ways, he had had an easy life, and he brought a long cultivated love of leisure to the golf course.

One day Mike came to a crossroads. He was in the pro shop, looking at some new lightweight jackets, when he overheard two men trying to arrange for their game. The course was booked up and allowing only foursomes for the rest of the day. Mike was there with his friend Frank and, without thinking much about it, asked the two men if they'd like to join him and Frank. They were a twosome, and they, too, were trying to find a way to get on the course.

The strangers were grateful and introduced themselves as Edward and Mephisto. Edward was a nervous sort, forever rubbing the back of his head when he spoke, as if he were never certain about what he said or whether he had the permission to say it. He was thin and blond and hovered around his friend like a servant. Mephisto was thin and tall, with shiny black hair, oiled close to his head, and a dark complexion.

"Mephisto? Is that a stage name? Surely it's not your real name," Mike said in the friendly way new golf partners banter at the beginning of a round.

"No, it's my name. My mother gave it to me." Mephisto pulled a wrinkled sheet of paper from his pocket. "Look here. My birth certificate. It proves I was born."

Mike was taken aback by the quick presentation of such a formal document over such a casual remark. "I didn't mean . . ."

The four men gathered their gear and headed toward the first tee, which was well over a hundred yards from the shop. Edward lagged behind, dragging a black golf bag the size of a small wardrobe.

"We usually like a small wager. Would you care to participate?" Mephisto said in a friendly tone that nevertheless reminded Mike of Bela Lugosi, perhaps the classic embodiment of Count Dracula, inviting a young woman to dinner.

He felt a chill at the suggestion, but he didn't want to be a prude, so he answered, "Well, we don't usually make bets on our game, but if it's modest, I'm willing."

"Fine by me," said Frank.

"I was thinking . . . one hundred dollars?" said Mephisto.

"Ooh, that's a bit steep," said Mike. "How about fifty?"

"Seventy-five?"

Mike and Frank agreed to the compromise.

At the first tee, Mephisto marched right up and placed his ball. He reached into the cavernous black bag and pulled out the most massive driver Mike had ever seen. Frank and Mike looked at each other, as if to say, "What have we got ourselves into?"

Mephisto took a hard, rough swing at the ball. It spun away from his club, making an odd buzzing noise. Mike noticed that the cover had split and was coming off. The ball thudded down some 50 yards.

Mike didn't venture a comment but only watched while the sinewy dark man set up a new ball. "Those cheap balls are good only for amateurs," he growled.

"A softer swing . . ." Frank began. Mephisto glared at him with such hostility that Frank's words buzzed out much the way the ball had done.

Edward, who had been quiet up to this time, spoke in a pinched voice. "Why don't you and Frank tee off after Mephisto?"

Mephisto stood at his teed-up ball once more and swung no less viciously. But this time he must have hit the sweet spot, if such a thing could ever be associated with him, and the ball simply disappeared into the sky. He didn't watch it but just walked off the tee box and tended to the black bag.

The other three hit ordinary tee shots and headed for the fairway.

On the green, Frank and Edward were putting for bogey, but Mephisto and Mike had a chance at birdies. For some reason unknown to him, Mike wanted to show "the Transylvanian"—as he now silently called Mephisto—that he could play golf well, and he wanted badly to make this putt.

"Let's make a deal," Mephisto said quietly to him with words considerably oiled. "I ask for your attention later to a plan I want to propose. In return for your promise to listen to me, just to listen to me, I'll square it with the laws of physics to make this putt of yours go in. But, if you don't agree, I assure you the ball won't come close to the hole, even for a par."

Mike took a step back. "You have that much control of the game?"

"That much," Mephisto hissed.

"Well, I think I'll test that power in a way that will benefit me rather than penalize me." Mike said lightly. "All right, I agree to listen."

"Good," said Mephisto. "Don't forget you agreed. Now take your birdie."

Mike studied his shot carefully. It was long, and the green had three plateaus, banking in various directions, between the ball and the hole. Never in a thousand years could he make this putt. He swung his putter carefully, and the ball rolled and curved and picked up speed and slowed down and finally plopped noisily into the hole. Mike smiled with delight. Mephisto's smile was less innocent.

At the second tee Mephisto once again demolished the ball with his awkward muscled swing. He placed a new ball on the tee. "I'm having trouble finding the rhythm," he said. He swung fiercely at the new ball, lost control, and banged it deep into the ground. He walked away in a rage.

"It's all right, Mr. Mephisto," Frank said. "Most golfers lose their temper sometime."

Edward shot a look at Frank in warning, but it was too late. Mephisto turned and hurled a golf ball at Frank. Everyone ducked. Mephisto calmly dusted his hands on his pants and made a comment about the beauty of the fairway. Mike nodded vigorously at Frank, who looked aghast and motioned for him to tee up. All four hit their balls moderately well and went off, each in his own direction, on the fairway. At the green, while waiting for Frank to hole out, Mike asked Mephisto about the deal he had spoken of. The volatile man spoke quietly: "We have to get to know each other better. On the back nine we'll talk about it."

Mike had his doubts that they would ever make it to the back nine, the way things were going. On the way to the third tee, a panicked Frank sidled up to Mike. "Who are these guys? They look like morticians on the job. Give me the creeps."

"I know. Mephisto's insane and Edward is probably a psychopath. Let's be careful. We can always call it quits after nine."

But the third and fourth holes were surprisingly normal. Only on the fifth hole was there reason for worry.

Again on the green, Mephisto made a remarkable putt from about 20 feet. "Well, now, I guess the hole is mine. That's four out of five at $75. Let's see. That's 300. I'm doing fairly well."

"What do you mean?" said Frank, unsettled.

"Our little wager. $75 per hole. Remember?" Mephisto said with a smile that revealed stained and uneven teeth.

"I thought you meant $75 for the game, eighteen holes," Mike said.

Mephisto reached into his pocket and pulled out a small shiny object. "I have it here on the recorder," he said with a note of triumph. "$75 for an entire game would not even be a bet. I believe that the authorities in the clubhouse would accept this tape as verification of the wager."

"But," moaned Frank, "that's $1,350 for eighteen."

"Only if you lose every hole. It could be worth over a thousand dollars to you. Who knows?" Mephisto laughed heartily. "Come on, boys, let's enjoy the game. Don't be worrywarts."

On the tenth tee, the game took a turn for the better, in some ways. Mephisto hit first, as usual, and delivered the ball on a low arc right onto the green 300 yards away. Mike was astonished. "Could you teach me how to do that?" he asked.

"That's nothing. I can teach you a lot more. But you have to understand my game. I play a special kind of golf. I'm not an innocent like you. If you give me something I want, I'll teach you more about golf than you ever imagined learning."

"What do I have that you could possibly want?" Mike said with some despair.

Mephisto looked closely into Mike's eyes. "You have a few things. For example, I'll teach you how to drive like that if you teach me about the physiology of the heart. You said you are a doctor, did you not?"

"That sounds like a good trade," Mike said innocently. "But why do you want to know?"

"In my business, it helps to know some anatomy and especially the pathways of the blood. I'm quite interested in blood."

"By the way, what is your business?"

"Oh, I'm in sales," Mephisto replied.

Mike told Mephisto everything he knew about the heart, or at least everything he could fit in between golf strokes. On the eleventh hole Mephisto handed Mike his oversized driver. "Just swing away with this club. Don't think about anything. Forget everything you've learned."

Mike stood at the tee and swung the heavy club naturally and unconsciously, and his ball flew off into the air and landed with a high bounce and trickled up onto the green 325 yards away. Mike was beside himself. He had never hit a ball that far and onto the green. Mephisto roared with laughter. Frank was dumbfounded, and Edward shook his head in a sad and knowing way as though he had some secret knowledge about what was unfolding on the course—and he did.

Mike fairly danced the length of the fairway, so delighted was he with his drive. Mephisto jogged to keep up with him, all the while asking him details about which rib marked the area where one had best access to the heart. Mike tried to take Mephisto's questions seriously, but his mind was on his glorious future in golf. He had finally broken the barrier of mediocrity.

On the green the stakes went up slightly. Mephisto's ball was on the edge of the green, in some light rough. Mike's was farther from the hole on the opposite side of the green. A steep slope and then a knobby ridge stood between him and the hole.

Mephisto put on his smile once again.

"You really enjoy this game, don't you, Mike? I suspect you wouldn't mind being a golfer full time, on the tour maybe."

"I'd love that," Mike admitted. But as he looked at the impossible putt in front of him, he felt doubtful.

"I have in my bag a putter that I have not used in this game. I save it for special occasions. It has never missed a putt in four years. It must be a magical tool. I don't understand it. I'll make a gift of it to you and ask only one thing in return."

"I'm a trained scientist," Mike replied. "There's no way I could believe in a magic putter."

"I don't ask you to. I only tell you that it has never missed a putt in four years of regular use. I don't know why it has this power, but my eyes have seen it. But if you are not interested . . ."

"Wait. I'm interested. Only skeptical. What do you want from me?"

"Your friendship. That's all. I see the way you look at me. Yes, I have a temper, but ask Edward. I control it most of the time. I'm not so bad. If you could find it in you just to try to like me, I'll give you the putter. I just want your promise."

Mike hesitated. He had an optimistic and forgiving nature. On the other hand, the elation he felt at making that stupendous drive was tempered by a growing sense that there was something dark, almost evil, surrounding this game. Edward was such a simp and appeared to be in Mephisto's control. Mike didn't want to risk that fate as well. But in the end, his good nature prevailed.

"All right, Mephisto," Mike said with a light laugh. "I'll try to be more open to you."

"Exactly what I want."

Mephisto then pulled a beautiful putter out of his bag and handed it to Mike. It had a tawny leather grip and polished shaft that sparkled in the sunlight. The hosel gleamed a golden color. Mike wondered if it could possibly be real gold. When Mike held the club and swung it lightly to get its feel, he was astonished. It was neither light nor heavy, neither awkward nor too easy. As a scientist, he rarely used the word *perfect,* but this club was indeed perfection.

"Why don't you try it? There's no one behind us. Putt a few balls for practice."

Mike dropped three balls on the edge of the green and hit them, one after the other, into the hole. He hit another with one hand and another behind his back. They all went in at about 20 feet. He laughed.

"Where did you get this?" he asked.

Mephisto answered quietly. "Perhaps when we get to know each other better, I'll tell you the story. It's a very interesting one. Quite unbelievable."

They went on with the game, and for the next several holes Mike never missed a putt, as long as the ball was on the green. He would rather have been given a skill than a trick iron, but it looked as if the relationship with Mephisto might be a long and positive one. There would doubtless be more benefits along the way, and Mephisto didn't ask for much in return.

On the twelfth hole, Mike saw Edward pass what looked like a packet of pills to Mephisto. Indigestion, perhaps. *Wouldn't it be nice,* he thought, *to have someone catering to your every need?*

After seeing Mike putt yet another hole in one stroke, Edward spoke up.

"I'm a dead man," he said.

"What? Oh, you mean because of my game," said Mike.

Edward reached the hole in three. "Our Mephisto is . . . How can I put this delicately? He's not quite normal. Prone to fits as you can probably imagine—brimstone, sulfur, horns—that sort of thing."

"You're not making any sense," Mike said, suddenly feeling like defending Mephisto.

"Golf brings out the deep dark passions in people. Don't be fooled into thinking that Mephisto here is everything he says he is." Edward said, his face growing even paler. "Keep your eyes open."

Frank had observed the discussion between Mike and Edward and he took Mike aside and asked him about it.

"It's pathetic," Mike said. "Edward compares himself to Mephisto and sees himself as being nothing. Nothing. And he has to try to drag Mephisto down."

"He seems like an ordinary person to me," said Frank.

They played the back 9 much better than the front and finally arrived at 18. The foursome ahead of them had slowed down. As they settled in for a wait, Mephisto took Mike to a shady grotto amid the trees, not far from the tee but out of earshot of Frank and Edward.

"This is it," said Mephisto. "It all comes down to this. I'm going to make you an offer. I want you to think about it carefully. Think about your dreams for your future. Think about a family you may have someday. Think about making a contribution to the world."

"I'm thinking," said Mike, not taking Mephisto too seriously.

"I am prepared to give you five million dollars plus a stellar career in professional golf."

"Five million dollars," Mike said with awe. "You aren't serious."

"I'm deadly serious."

"What do you want in return?"

"Not much really. In fact, for you it may be nothing at all."

"Well, what is it?"

"I want your soul."

Mike looked stunned and confused. "My soul. What is that? And how can I give it to you?"

"Here's where the scientist you are may judge me foolish. All you need to do is sign a contract I have prepared. It indicates that upon your signature your soul is mine, and the money and skills are yours."

"But I don't believe in a soul. The paper would be worthless."

"Let me decide that," said Mephisto spreading out a piece of paper on a large rock. He took a pen from his pocket and offered it to Mike.

"This is archaic," Mike protested. "No one today sells his soul. It sounds like some old story."

"It's fine if you think that way. In fact, it's better. You don't give up anything this way. You just humor me and sign the contract."

"Tell me this. Honestly. Can a person sell his soul?"

Mephisto looked very serious, sad even. "People sell their souls to corporations, political parties, religious institutions, in marriage. They surrender themselves to someone else or to some goal they have been convinced is worthy. People sell their souls every day, but they don't do it for real profit. If you don't sell your soul to me, you'll probably sell it to someone else pretty soon."

"What happens to these people who sell their souls without a contract?" Mike asked. He was whispering now.

"They get sick or divorced. They lose their jobs. They get depressed. They drink or they work too much."

"Doesn't sound good," Mike responded.

"No, it doesn't. But I'm only asking you to sign a paper, not to get divorced and all the rest. Surely you don't believe that by putting your name on a piece of paper, all these bad things are going to happen to you."

"Absolutely I don't," said Mike the scientist.

"But you do believe, don't you, that I am going to give you the money and the career."

"I do," said Mike. "I don't know why, but I'm sure you can keep your promises."

"Good. Then just sign your name."

Mike took the pen. At that moment Edward walked over to them. "We need to finish up this game and go." For the first time he put his hand on Mephisto's arm as if to pull him away. Then he saw the pen in Mike's hand and the paper. "No. Don't sign that. You don't want to sign anything without at least reading it carefully."

Mephisto was still for a moment. He looked closely at Mike. Then he said, "Edward, you're right, as always. Mike, you should think carefully. You could be making a big mistake."

Mephisto's even-tempered reaction to Edward sealed the deal and Mike signed his name with a flourish.

Six months later Frank found himself at the golf course, sitting at the bar in the clubhouse. He felt someone shift into the seat next to him and then heard a familiar voice. It was Edward's.

"Frank, how are you doing?" he said in a friendly tone.

"Edward, I haven't seen you since . . ."

"I know. How's our mutual friend, Mike?"

"It's a sad story. That check of Mephisto's was obviously a fake—even Mike knew that. But soon after that he came into some real money—an inheritance, I think. He lost most of it within six months. And the day after we played golf together he found a mole on his shoulder. Melanoma. He's lost his job at the research institute, and he's seeing a psychiatrist and a bevy of doctors. Very sad."

"I was afraid something like that would happen."

"Well, I blame that devil of a friend of yours."

"Oh, he's no devil. He's just not quite himself. I don't think I told you: I'm a psychiatric nurse at the mental health institute down the road. Sometimes we take a patient to the course. It's good for them—the exercise, fresh air, sport, a little contact with people."

"Did Mike know about this? Who you are? Who was Mephisto?"

"You mean Mr. Delaney. Calls himself a lot of names, big names—Nero, Hitler, Gandhi. No, I don't remember telling Mike. I thought you would both figure it out. But I did try to break it up when Mr. Delaney got Mike off in a corner. Delusional people can be very convincing."

"Is he ever benevolent?"

"Oh, yes, he can do Jesus Christ quite well, and Martin Luther."

"I wonder," Frank said, "if Mr. Delaney could help Mike now. He needs a strong positive jolt. Do you think he'd be up for another round of golf? I'd arrange it with Mike."

Edward rubbed the back of his head, a gesture that now looked like deep thought rather than nervousness. "Mr. Delaney is more inclined to play the angel these days. It's worth a try. You never know about the power of words."

CHAPTER 15

Cosmic Golf

Sixteen-year-old Robbie Portman sat hunched on the front steps of the house in which he had recently moved with his mother and father and younger sister. He hadn't wanted to leave Chicago for the East Coast; now he would have to discover a whole new world and new people. Didn't his family realize that he was not born with the talents for such immense projects?

"Sulking won't help," his father, James, said, walking past him down the steps to their white sedan parked on the opposite side of the street near the course. "It's your life," he called out as he drove away. Grumpily Robbie got to his feet, as if determined to now prove to his father that yes, it was his life, and nothing would come of it. He set off for the corner only dimly aware of the city golf course on the opposite side of the narrow street. Robbie walked for the rest of the afternoon. Pigeons, cars, people hurrying past, only one pizza parlor; life was going to be grim.

He returned home at dusk, this time noticing the few diehards still on the golf course; the deep green of the fifth fairway stretched the 300 yards between the busy intersection with Main Street and their house. He climbed the steps, took one last look at the town he had been exiled to, and noticed a tall, thin golfer at the fifth tee. The man's shirt was a shimmering charcoal color and reached almost to his knees. He wore loose fitting gray satiny pants. Robbie, who knew little about golf, still recognized the man's swing as one of great beauty, the ball arcing high into the darkening sky, and he couldn't help but nod his head in affirmation and admiration.

The next morning Robbie was sitting at the breakfast table slapping his spoon into a bowl of mashed fruit and muesli when, through the window, he noticed that same man taking aim on the fifth tee and once more hitting a high, arcing ball that seemed to disappear in the heavens. His father stood at the counter making toast.

"Dad, look at that golfer. His swing is amazing. How does he do it?"

"Didn't know you liked golf," his dad said, glancing up.

"I don't. I don't like it at all. I hate living across from that ugly course. I'd rather see a gas station."

His dad buttered his toast and sat down at the table. "You'll adjust," he said. "You'll have to."

Robbie dumped his bowl in the sink and stalked out the front door. The golfer was still there, the sunlight bouncing off his long gray shirt. Robbie crossed the street and stood close to the row of low bushes separating the public walk from the course.

After the man hit another lofting ball he turned around and spoke to Robbie.

"Would you be my caddie? I'll pay you fifty dollars for nine holes. I need help."

Robbie laughed. "You don't look like you need help with your game."

"No, I need a different kind of help. Mainly conversation. But you could carry my clubs."

Robbie glanced back at his house. What if his father was watching and saw that he was actually enjoying himself? After a moment's hesitation he said, "Okay. Once. Nine holes. Fifty bucks."

They walked toward the sixth hole and Robbie noticed that the man either had a limp or a stiff leg, maybe two stiff legs. He walked strangely; he was straight like a telephone pole. When he bent over the ball, his back formed a perfect line, and yet his swing was silky and relaxed.

The golf bag was surprisingly light, and when Robbie made mention of it, the man said, "I got those clubs back home. They make them so that you can carry them. We don't use carts where I come from."

"Oh," said Robbie.

They walked in silence for a while, and then Robbie noticed the man's shoes were a luminous gray like his shirt. "Where do you get your shoes and shirt? Do you mind my asking?"

"Not at all. I get those at home, too. We like fabrics that are light and soft on our skin. The same goes for shoes. I can't wear the clothes you have around here."

Robbie looked down at his shock absorbing, Velcro sneakers with their blue stripes. "I guess you're right. They are a bit—bulky."

The man reached for an iron and sent the ball sailing down the fairway. The swish of the club was so soft that Robbie felt hypnotized by the sheer sound of it.

"Would you like to learn how to play?"

Robbie suddenly wondered if he should have joined up with this man. After all, he was a stranger. But then Robbie decided to have a little faith. Wasn't he supposed to be exploring his new world, meeting people? "Sure. But I want to play the way you do."

"I'll show you. We've developed a plan of learning that's painless and quick."

"Who's we?"

"I mean my countrymen. But I'll tell you all about that later." He glanced around. "Here, you can use my clubs. It's against the rules here, but we're pretty much alone on the course today."

The two went on playing from hole to hole. Robbie was shocked at how quickly he got into the game. The swish of his iron shots was almost as remarkable as those of his companion.

When they finished the ninth hole, the man asked if Robbie would like to play another nine holes. They could rent some clubs for him. Delighted, Robbie agreed. Before starting the back nine, the man offered to buy Robbie lunch at the club shop. He ordered a salad without any dressing and a glass of water; Robbie asked for a ham sandwich and a Coke. They sat at a small table in the corner and ate.

"Do you miss Chicago?" the man said.

Robbie frowned. "I didn't tell you I'm from Chicago. How do you know?"

The man sat a tad straighter in his chair. "Robbie, I guess I should now tell you a little about me. There's nothing to worry about. I may have a job for you."

"But how do you know where I come from?" Robbie persisted.

"It's a long and complicated story, and you'll have trouble believing it. Before I tell it, let me assure you that I am completely sane and mentally fit."

This unsettled Robbie. He looked around and saw, thankfully, that the shop was full of ordinary-looking people.

"My name is Coeli. That's with a *C*. It sounds like the Irish name Kelly except the *e* is a little broader. By the way, I know that your mother is from Ireland. Coeli's not my real name. You couldn't pronounce my family name." He paused. "I come from a planet belonging to a star you can see with your naked eye on a clear night."

The oddest thing, Robbie would recall years later, was his sudden and surging desire to believe the man. A visitor from another planet? Yes, it could be. He seemed like such an intelligent and refined person and Robbie couldn't bear to doubt him. When the short moustached man from the counter came over to the table and greeted Robbie, it was confirmation of a sort. "New here, aren't you? I see you've made a friend of our local alien. Don't worry, he's harmless. Well, welcome."

"Thanks," Robbie said quietly. The counter man went back to refilling the saltshakers.

Coeli said, "You see? I tell everyone where I come from, and no one believes me. They think I'm loony and humor me and leave me alone. But I'm deadly serious."

Robbie's heart was beating fast. "Why did you pick me? You picked me, didn't you?"

"Yes, we picked you. My associates and I. We arranged for the move from Chicago because this golf course is our best staging area on Earth. Please believe me. This is very serious business."

"I'm trying," Robbie said.

"That's all I can ask. Let me explain just a few things. Would you like another Coke?"

Robbie shook his head.

"All right. We've had discussions in our community about Earth. It's a beautiful planet, and so far the myriad of cultures on it have been evolving rather successfully. But now you are reaching a turning point. You must either mature rapidly or self-destruct. We see serious signs of global failure." Coeli spoke of inequality in the distribution of resources that would lead to even more conflicts and wars. He spoke of the proliferation of weapons and widespread suffering. "But with all of this, you have wonderful arts, athletics, and growing movements toward maturity. Some of us are in favor of intervention and some think we have no business interfering. My being here lets you know where I stand."

"But what does golf have to do with any of this?" Robbie asked.

"Good question, though not the first I would ask. It's all about the design of the golf course and the way the game is played. Semiotically, it reproduces certain mathematical features of the cosmos. We recognize golf courses on planet Earth as signs of peaceful intent and pleasure in life. We see people enjoying themselves, not working so hard. In our way of life, play is more important than work. These are all signals of an advanced civilization."

"Golf tells you that we're advanced?"

"We play what is essentially the same game on our planet. Of course, as I said, we have more comfortable clothes and lighter clubs."

"Well, you're an advanced civilization."

"Ah, belief," Coeli said with a smile. "It waxes and wanes."

"Give me some time. And tell me more about golf," Robbie said.

"In Gematria—that's a symbolic system of numbers—eighteen is the number of life. In golf the player advances through eighteen fairways, or life paths, dealing with all kinds of symbolic hazards, aiming for the least effort in strokes. That's a perfect model for life. The green grass represents the field on which life is played out. From where I live, those fairways and greens all over the planet are impressive."

"So golf is a sign of our advanced civilization?"

"Relatively speaking. You're more advanced than some planets, less than others. We're a long way ahead."

"And why me?"

"You're open, intelligent, well balanced, and normal." Robbie felt himself blushing. "We think you can help us get the message to the planet about growing up and making better choices. We want to see you working together as a planetary community."

"What do I do?"

Here Coeli squirmed a little in his chair, showing the first sign of unease.

"I'd like to take you to my home—for just a while—to get some training. Then you'll know what to do to help us and help your people."

"Okay . . . and how do we get to your place?"

"That's something I can't begin to describe to you. We're just way ahead in the transportation field. No wheels. No rockets. And it's completely safe."

"You want me to visit your planet?"

"Take it as an invitation. If you don't want to come, of course you don't have to. From our planet, with a small amateur telescope, you look at Earth and you see brilliant dots of green everywhere—golf courses. Come, let's finish our game."

Later that afternoon Robbie ran up the steps to find his parents and his sister in the living room.

"Robbie!" His mother embraced him. "I was starting to worry."

"Not me," said his sister. "I wasn't."

"You won't believe this." Robbie wriggled out of his mother's arms. "I met a man, a very nice man, a very intelligent man. He taught me some golf and now he wants me to get some training where he lives."

"What kind of training, son?" his father asked. He held a painting up to the wall while Robbie's sister gauged if it was straight.

"Training for world peace, Dad. He wants me to help him mature planet Earth. We'll help the environment, work for an equal distribution of resources, and of course give the arts a boost."

"Why, that sounds grand," his mother said with pride.

"I didn't know you were interested in these things," his father said.

"What's the catch?" his sister added.

Robbie closed his eyes. "He's from another planet."

"He must be," said his father. "You'd have to have a big imagination to do all that."

"No, I mean he really is from another planet, a real planet."

The family suddenly became quiet.

"He wants me to go to his planet to train."

More silence.

"You talked this all over on the golf course?" His father leaned the painting against the wall.

"Yes. I have to admit it sounds strange, maybe unbelievable," Robbie answered.

"I'll go upstairs and knit you a space suit," his sister said.

"Wait. Coeli warned me it might be difficult to convince you that he's real. He's offered to come and talk to you. Can we invite him to dinner?"

"A Kelly?" said his mother. "Of course, we'll have him come for dinner."

"What sort of nutritional units does he consume?" the sister asked.

"He's really nice," said Robbie. "He might even convince you. I'm not completely convinced myself, but I'm about seventy-five percent sure."

Somehow it was agreed that Coeli would come to dinner on the following Saturday. In the meantime, Robbie continued to caddie for him. Following him around the course, Robbie learned that Coeli played a beautiful game and enjoyed it thoroughly, but he didn't keep score and wouldn't have scored low if he did keep track.

"A game like golf is a preparation for life. You don't need so much competition and goal setting in life, so it's not good to put too much stock in golf. Relax and play the game. Once in a while I enjoy a good match, and then I try to score well. But I like a proportion of about a hundred to one."

Robbie wasn't quite sure what Coeli was talking about, but his admiration for the alien grew every day. By the time Coeli came to dinner, Robbie's belief was almost complete.

Coeli arrived dressed in the same clothes he always wore. They didn't need to be washed, he explained once to Robbie; it had something to do with the material. He had a bottle in his hand and gave it to Robbie's mother at the door.

"Vinegar," she said. "How nice."

"Isn't that what you traditionally bring to dinner?" he asked.

"Usually it's wine, but this is fine. We can use it, to be sure."

"I always get those mixed up," Coeli said. He laughed and walked into a bedroom off the foyer.

When they had settled around the table for supper, Coeli asked if he could offer a prayer. He stood on his chair and raised his arms and began a lovely chant in a strange language. Afterward, they dug into their meal.

"Maybe Robbie told you my plans for him," Coeli said.

Robbie's mother said, "Indeed he has. But to be honest, it all sounds a bit strange."

"Of course it does," said Coeli. "It's not every day that you have an alien sitting at dinner with you and asking to take your son millions of miles away for two weeks."

"Two weeks?" his sister half screamed. "I thought it would be a few hours. Isn't that what abductees say?"

Coeli looked mildly indignant. "I have no intention of abducting your brother and son, believe me. In fact, I will take him only if the whole family agrees with the plan. His sister as well. There must be consensus."

"Where would he be going?" the father asked.

"In all modesty, I must tell you that I have a very special job in my community. I am the Secretary of Alien Civilizations. Imagine that. And my mother always thought I wouldn't amount to anything."

"I don't think we have that position here," said Robbie's mother.

"I will take him to our government headquarters, where we will train him in interplanetary peace protocols. IPP. We know how to accelerate education, so we can give him what you refer to as a Ph.D. after the two weeks. But it won't be all work. We have excellent four-dimensional golf courses. We'll teach him the game and he can play whenever he needs some relaxation."

"What happens when he returns?"

"Very interesting," said Coeli. "I explained to Robbie that cultures are not all equal in their cultural evolution, and those of us who have solved most of our problems have debated whether we should intervene or not when a society is becoming outrageously dangerous, as Earth is today. We have decided to try to influence your society in a positive way, partnering with a few select Earth people. We like the idealism and energy of the youth especially. When Robbie returns, he will work for cultural development with the knowledge and skills we have given him. He will even be able to continue to communicate with us, though we have to leave the planet soon. I am not allowed to take a personal role but can work only from a distance. I will leave a piece of crystal that will facilitate our communications." He turned to Robbie's mother. "It's a beautiful piece. Quite large. You could display it."

"Are there more of you on Earth now?" the sister asked.

"Yes, a few, on golf courses here and there."

"I don't know what to think," Robbie's father said.

Robbie's mother seemed quite taken with Coeli and she ushered him into the living room, where she served coffee and cake. "It hasn't been easy on Robbie and his sister to relocate," she said.

"I know. But we have arranged for Robbie's father to get a significant promotion. Any time after Robbie returns you may go back to Chicago, but I have a feeling that you're going to like it here, especially when Robbie teaches you our form of golf. The course across the street is a major interplanetary stopover."

Robbie's sister gave Coeli a questioning look and his father coughed.

"May I play a song for you?" Coeli asked. "We need to relax after all of these plans and revelations." He reached into a pocket and withdrew a tiny piece of metal with a wire string just three inches long attached to it. He struck the string with his thumb and a rich, warm sound filled the room. When he sang in his language, the family fell into a deep trance that lasted an hour. They all woke up at the same time, refreshed.

"Would you mind playing that tune once more?" James asked.

"We have a problem with music addiction in our society. I wouldn't want to seed that here on Earth."

"I have one more question," James said. He paused for a minute. "I don't like to ask this, but how do we know you're not a nut?"

"A fair question," said Coeli. "I don't know how to assure you that I'm bona fide." He pronounced it "bow-nah fih-day." "You'll have to take your chances."

After church the next morning, Robbie went to the course to play a full game with Coeli.

"How do you think it went with your parents?" Coeli asked as they teed up.

"I don't know. I think half of them thought you were nuts and half the genuine article."

"Are you counting your sister?"

"Yes."

"So one of them is split both ways."

"Something like that," said Robbie, who then made a lovely whoosh with his six iron.

An attendant drove by on a golf cart full of shovels and hoes.

"Hey Coeli," he shouted and stopped the cart. "Where's your friend from?"

"Oh, he's from Earth. Robbie, meet Globus. He's one of my countrymen. There are two of us on this course." Then he spoke to Globus. "Are there any other visitors here?"

"Yes, counting members of the local club, we have about ten. This course is becoming quite the hot spot, you know. They're from everywhere."

"We'll have to be careful. Someone might catch on to us."

Globus grinned. "If anyone gets suspicious about one of us, I just tell them the guy's not right in the head or that he's an escapee from the mental hospital."

He waved good-bye and sped off in the golf cart, holding onto the wheel with stiff-looking arms.

Robbie asked, "Do you mean there are aliens all over this course?"

"A few. By the way, *aliens* is a term of disrespect. We prefer *visitors*."

"And you all want to play golf?"

"Of course. People enjoy golf throughout the galaxy. This planet-centered idea that you invented the game—in Scotland, is it?—is just a sign that you haven't matured yet. As I've explained, a golf course has certain mathematical, navigational, and mystical properties that appeal to visitors, not to mention the aesthetics. If you visit I'll show you my telescope that highlights all the courses on earth; it sort of lights them up. It's quite a sight. I find it very moving and inspiring."

They finished nine holes and arrived back at the clubhouse to find Robbie's father pacing back and forth in front of the bar. "Can I get you a drink?" he said to Coeli.

"My system can't tolerate alcohol, but I'll have some beet juice if they have it."

James, who joined them in the clubhouse, asked the bartender to serve his son a Coke and Coeli something red.

"Look," he said, settling onto a barstool. "I believe in you, and I want the best for my son. Especially now he needs something to inspire him. You can have him for two weeks. We have a consensus. But we want him back. My wife has her doubts, and my daughter, well she thinks you're a little crazy. But they love Robbie and they believe in your philosophy."

"Thank you for your trust, James. This could be important for all of us. We'll leave from the ninth green tomorrow morning and be back in exactly two weeks. You can meet us there, but don't stand on the green while you're waiting."

With that Coeli and a delighted Robbie went to finish their game. James ordered another drink.

The bartender set the Bloody Mary in front of him. "That guy's a mental case, but I think he's harmless. By the way, your son's game is improving nicely."

James blanched. "How do you know?" he asked.

"I get off early on Thursdays to play a round and I saw him—"

"No, no—you said the man he plays with has mental problems."

"That's what our new greenskeeper tells me," the bartender said as he topped off the bowls of pretzels on the bar. "You ready for another drink?"

CHAPTER 16

Peace and Tranquility

Night creates its own semblance of quiet, even on a crowded airplane, but Steven O'Malley couldn't sleep. The drone of the jet engines, the muffled squawk of movies playing in the seats across the aisle, the soft twitter of a conversation several rows behind him, each adding to a muted polyphony of excited souls that layered the air around him like a Palestrina motet.

The standard-issue blue blanket covered his shoulders and he pretended he was in bed, but the sharp edges of his thoughts kept him alert. It was 2 A.M. at home in Boston and the plane was somewhere over the middle of the Atlantic Ocean, rushing toward morning and a country he had long dreamed of but had never known in the flesh.

He had many things to think about: his marriage, looking doubtful, as he and Margie seemed to be moving in different directions. They both had wanted children, she more than Stephen, but the doctors were unanimous in urging them to adopt. Then there was the recent verdict from yet another team of doctors about his prostate and the bothersome increase of cancer cells. Finally, there was his job, perhaps the victim of the other two crises, on the block because of the many absences and missed meetings and botched deals over which Stephen seemed to have no control.

These three issues flailed in his head as he crunched into a seat obviously designed by the Marquis de Sade. He had never been to Ireland, the land of his ancestors, and was making the journey now only at the insistence of his wife, who hoped that a little distance might give them perspective, and of his boss, who suggested a rest. He had heard about Ireland's challenging and beautiful golf courses, so somewhere in the hold beneath his economy seat sat his clubs, ready for a little action on a course not far from Dublin.

Martin, the shrewd manager of his team at work, had been to Ireland and had told Stephen to prepare for a land of intelligent and strong-willed people and not the Hollywood stereotype of leprechauns and cute rosy-cheeked peasants. Stephen didn't know what to expect, but he hoped that the newness of the place might help him rearrange his thoughts and find a more optimistic approach to the depressing complexities of his life. Three doctors had recommended antidepressants, but he wasn't inclined to solve his problems with drugs, legal or otherwise.

A stranger in an unknown land without a partner, he wondered if he would enjoy golf on his own. Now more than ever he needed something pleasurable in his life. The plane skimmed low over impossibly green fields and touched down. Stephen moved quickly through customs, and was just exiting the baggage area, where he'd claimed his clubs, when a tall, wiry man with anarchic tufts of white hair on his long aquiline head approached him.

"You're very welcome to Ireland," he said to Stephen, shaking his hand and helping with the awkward carton of clubs.

"Thank you," said Stephen. "Did the company tell you I was coming?"

"And which company would that be, sir?" the man said with a smile.

"I think you may be mistaking me for someone else."

"Sure, you're the man named after Stephen martyr and are having a bit of a rough spot with your wife and your job."

"That's me," he said, momentarily taken aback by the man's candor. "Stephen martyr. Who sent you, then?"

The man darted about like a bird, helping Stephen gather his things, ignoring the question.

Stephen abandoned the task of unraveling the man's identity and simply let the stranger lead him out of the airport to the taxi rank, where he flagged down a large cab that could hold the clubs and luggage. Stephen noticed that the man had no suitcases or golf clubs of his own.

After securing Stephen in the backseat, the man closed the cab's door and walked back into the airport, leaving Stephen agape. He had supposed the man would have accompanied him to his hotel.

"The Great Northern in Wicklow," Stephen said to the driver, and they quickly moved away from the airport, through the congested streets of the city, and onto a wide highway that bore them toward a pointed hill called Sugarloaf.

After checking in, Stephen stored his clubs in a room just off reception at the hotel, and then went to his small suite overlooking the golf course. There was a light rain falling, but the concierge had assured him he would still get out on the links.

He tried to take a shower, to wash off the sticky feeling of the overnight flight, but he couldn't get any hot water. After a call to a helpful sweet lady at the desk, a young man came and gave him instructions on how to turn on the water heater shortly before a shower and then turn it off to conserve electricity. Stephen looked in wonder at the various switches and cords needed to take a simple shower.

In the hotel restaurant he ordered a traditional Irish breakfast, though his body wasn't ready for food, and he discovered that the sausage wasn't what he expected and so he opted for the buffet and had some scrambled eggs and raspberry yogurt, which was surprisingly creamy and flavorful. He sat at an out-of-the-way table and saw that there were other men, no doubt away on business, sitting alone, reading newspapers and drinking coffee or tea.

He was about to leave the breakfast room when he saw a familiar figure enter and look around. It was the man from the airport. His hair was still sticking straight up on his narrow head and he seemed even thinner and more animated. He spotted Stephen, came over, and sat down.

"Mr. O'Malley," he said with his usual smile. "A good morning to you. Did you get some sleep?"

"Not yet," said Stephen. "How did you know where I was, and who I was, for that matter?"

"Oh, of course I didn't," the man answered, "but Ireland is a small country. You'll have to get used to that."

Stephen didn't know what Ireland's being small had to do with this man just happening to walk into the room where Stephen was having breakfast, but he accepted the invitation not to inquire into mysteries beyond his powers. Ireland, he was already coming to believe, was stranger and maybe more enchanted than he had expected.

"I thought you might like a partner on the links. I don't play often, and I'm not as fit as you, but I enjoy the game. I've watched folk play often enough that I think I've the gist of the sport."

"Funny. I was just thinking about being alone here and needing someone to play with."

The man ignored Stephen's remark and went on to tell Stephen about Wicklow and the hotel and the golf course. It was built, he explained, over an area that was once protected by the local people because of its holy wells and sacred stones. There had been some protests, when the golf course was first proposed, but practicality and economic lure won out over superstition and the hotel complex went up quickly. "Still," the man cautioned, "one must be careful about certain areas of the course."

Stephen had no idea what the man was talking about, but he made the appropriate polite remarks about being careful.

After breakfast, Stephen went to his room, had three hours of sleep and then got ready for the game. He put on his golf attire, retrieved his clubs, and met his white-haired friend at the golf office, where he was huddling with an older man Stephen had seen at the reception desk when he arrived.

"I'm afraid I didn't get your name," Stephen said to his new companion.

"Call me Fergus," the man said, laughing, as if he found his own name amusing.

They headed out toward the golf course, and at the lower entrance of the clubhouse, a teenage boy appeared with Fergus's equipment: a large, beautifully made bag, loaded with clubs and attached to a pull cart with large wheels that had shiny spokes and new tires.

The day was sunny but chilly, and Stephen felt comfortable in the warm woolen Donegal sweater he had bought at the hotel shop. The two men walked to the first tee with anticipation. "I'm happy to go first and give you a little taste of the course," Fergus said, and he walked directly to the tee and set up his golf ball. He took no practice swings but simply hit the ball with an unconventional, even awkward swing. The ball sailed off straight and high and ended up in the center of the fairway.

Stephen was still sleepy from the night flight and the change of time, and he swung at the ball too hard, his body completely out of position. His ball rolled into a clump of trees in the high rough. As he walked into the tall grass, Fergus came over to him and said, "Why don't you hit another ball from the fairway?"

"I can hit from the rough," Stephen countered a bit defensively.

"To be sure you can, but this is one of those places I was telling you about. A fairy fort. It's bad luck to go into them. I know it's an old superstition, but I think we shouldn't take any chances."

Stephen shrugged his shoulders, and walked back to the fairway and hit another ball.

"They'll be thanking you kindly," said Fergus.

The second and third holes were uneventful. Stephen got back into stride and hit the ball better. Fergus played magnificently yet with consistently bad form.

When they arrived at the fourth hole, a short par three, Fergus said, "I suggest you use an old ball on this hole. Nothing too expensive."

"Why? It's a short hole. Chances are, I won't lose a ball here."

"Whatever you say," Fergus answered. He swung and his ball landed on the green, on the far edge. Stephen also made the green in one, and the two walked the short distance to their balls.

"This used to be sacred ground," Fergus reminded him. "Some people believe there are still remnants here and there of the ancient magic, and this fourth hole is a good example. So be careful, please."

"Of course," said Stephen. He didn't want to look like a skeptical foreigner unwilling to adopt the ways of the country. He watched Fergus hit his ball into the hole from a considerable distance and noticed that he didn't bother to retrieve it. Then Stephen hit his ball. It followed a mysterious twisting path across the undulating grass and plopped in. Stephen knelt at the hole, but he couldn't reach his ball.

"I don't understand," he told Fergus. "The hole's too deep. Would you mind giving it a try?"

"I've got long fingers to be sure, but not that long," said Fergus. "They say some of the holes here reach right down to the earth's core. You can see some of them steaming on a cool morning."

"You don't believe that, do you?" said Stephen.

"Not at all, sir. I don't believe any of it. All the same, I can't reach your ball. I warned you."

Stephen pushed his putter, butt end first, into the hole and it went in up to the head of the club.

"I've never seen anything like this," said Stephen. "But I've been warned about the extravagant wit of the Irish. This must raise a good laugh when you locals watch Americans try to fetch their balls. It's like a birthday candle you can't blow out."

"Sometimes I think that the land is a bit wittier than the people are," Fergus responded. "I would definitely not put my foot into that hole."

Stephen humored him and walked off to the next tee.

On the fifth hole, Stephen was standing at the tee, surveying the unfamiliar layout of the fairway and hazards, when a strong wind came up suddenly. He lost his footing and fell on the tee, and his visor flew off and blew away so fast he hadn't a chance to retrieve it.

Fergus frowned. "That was an unusual little twister that blew up for you, sir. I'd say that the spirits of the place are pleased with you. Maybe they'll help your game."

Sure enough, when Stephen finally hit his drive on the long hole, the ball shot into the air and seemed to be borne on a fast cloud over several hazards to the edge of the green more than 300 yards away. He was looking pleased with his shot.

Fergus said, "Good indeed, but the winds should get the credit for that shot, sir."

Stephen thought he saw Fergus make a small gesture with his hands. Fergus then took his turn, and again a strong wind blew out of nowhere, taking the ball far left into a patch of heather and rocks.

"Do you mind if I hit another?" Fergus called out. "Those winds are playing with me."

"Of course," said Stephen. Then he definitely saw Fergus put his club on the ground and open his arms to the course in front of him and make a motion of calming. The winds died down.

"How do you do that?" he asked Fergus as they walked to the green.

"It's like calming your emotions and the flotsam of your life," he said. "You have to accept the authority and just do it."

"But we're playing golf."

"There's no *but* about it," Fergus said, spitting his *t*'s. "The next time the wind blows up, you try it. Use your arms. Calm the world around you. Golf is practice for life. If you can do it here, you can do it anywhere."

"Your name isn't Fergus, is it?"

"Why do you say that?"

"What is your real name?"

"I go by many names. I happen to like Fergus. I'm also known as Boreas."

"Fergus Boreas?"

"You could say that."

Fergus stood tall on the tee and took a deep breath. "Soon we will arrive at the back nine." The words sounded ominous. "You will have to be ready for that. Stand up here next to me on this rock and take a deep, deep breath."

Stephen stood next to Fergus on top of a boulder and looked out over the verdant expanse and the stately trees. They both breathed deeply.

"Good," said Fergus. "Now exhale, strongly."

Stephen let the air out of his lungs in a long, powerful breath.

"Breathing in and breathing out is the whole secret of life. Your actual breath, and the way you live. Take in, let go. Take in, let go."

Fergus motioned for Stephen to sit on the rock next to him.

"About this prostate," he said.

"Who told you about that?"

"The prostate controls semen and urine, and, think about it. Both of these fluids have to do with taking in and letting go. You hold your desire and then suddenly it rushes out as a fluid. You hold your liquid detritus, and suddenly it flows out. Apparently, there's something wrong in your holding in and letting go. We'll work on that, especially on the back nine. If you have the stomach for it."

Stephen stood up, a little miffed. It was all a touch too personal. "I really don't know what you're talking about. And what is this about the back nine? You make it sound like . . . like some kind of test . . ."

"You'll certainly need courage for it. On the back nine you'll confront the demons that have been ruining your life."

"But this is just a game. A game of golf."

"Indeed it is."

Fergus marched with long and rapid pace to the sixth hole. There he hit a long ball on a very long hole. He seemed to be gaining in stature and height and his skin had taken on a luminous glow.

"We have to build up steam for the back nine," he yelled to Stephen from the other side of the fairway. Stephen had hit a moderately long ball down the right side.

By the time they reached the ninth hole, a strange anarchy appeared to be overtaking their game. Shots were going wide and wild. Winds came up suddenly in the midst of calm. They died down just as quickly. A reddish hue tinted the cloudy sky. There were stretches of the course that barely looked maintained. They were playing in a wilderness, on a moor, an uncivilized patch of land at the whim of the sea. And Stephen felt caught up in the wild and transformative energy.

At the tenth hole, the world of the course seemed barely able to hold together. Stephen saw other golfers walking slanted into the bracing winds toward the clubhouse. Fergus looked frosty and windblown in both visage and form. He beckoned Stephen to the tee, a mere mound of rock surrounded by blond, blowing grasses. He had to shout, and his voice, hollow and whistling, seemed to come from a funnel in the very depths of his lungs.

"Hit the ball, Stephen," he bellowed. "You must play the game. Your soul is at stake."

Stephen felt the strong wind sting his face and hands, not from the cold as much from the power. He tried to hold his club, but the air rushed into his nose and mouth and he had trouble breathing and focusing on the game. His practice swings were wild as if he were swishing haphazardly at invisible obstacles. Sounds, too, assaulted him and added to the air of frenzy that surrounded him on all sides: the roar of winds, the bellow of trees. *Armageddon,* Stephen thought, *could be no worse.*

Somehow Stephen and Fergus managed to hole their balls on the smidgen of green. The din ceased and a hush came upon the course. Fergus beckoned Stephen to the eleventh tee, and Stephen cockily strutted up to it.

"I didn't think we'd ever survive the savagery of the tenth," he said.

Fergus frowned with his vast white hairy brows and said, "This is only the beginning, the mere commencement of the back nine. Don't go complacent on me," he said calmly.

They hit their tee shots and then pitched to the green. Everything appeared to be normal, but Fergus crouched when he walked, as though he expected wild beasts to appear at any second. They chipped to the green and readied for their putts.

"Be prepared," said Fergus.

Stephen shrugged his shoulders and hit his long putt. It was wide of the hole, but halfway there it cornered and headed straight for the target. Just before it would have sunk in the hole, a creature emerged. Slimy and serrated, it slithered out of the hole. It was half snake and half lizard, long and dark green, scaly and scabbed, dripping with a white syrupy sap that made Stephen nauseated. It headed quickly toward Fergus, who swore and deflected it with a swing of his wedge. Then it headed directly and swiftly to Stephen. Quickly he pulled out his five wood and used the best form in his arsenal to urge the demon back into its hole. He struck the sickening head time after time, until the beast began to weaken and finally inch back into its place of origin somewhere deep in the earth. Again a sudden quiet and peace settled on the green, and Stephen stood there with the wood in his hand as Fergus climbed back onto the low bent grass. Stephen noticed that, for all the battling, the carpet of the green still lay unblemished.

"I think we'll survive the back nine," Fergus said with a smile, clamping his large boney hand on Stephen's shoulder in a gesture of approval.

"Was that real?" Stephen asked. "Was I dreaming?"

"That beast was a real as anything in reality," Fergus answered. "Don't forget. You're in Ireland now, and this land is one of those remaining places on earth where the great spirits still show themselves and the mythological battles and loves play themselves out without any camouflage."

"But I was told that Ireland was entering the modern world," Stephen countered.

"It is, and we don't have much time left. Here, you can still hear the banshee cry. You can still heal your illnesses in holy wells set deep in the earth. And people, the old ones especially, still avail themselves of these preternatural resources. But that new Ireland, the one without the Irish spirit, will become a place like any other place, and the gateways to the realm of spirits will close over. But that isn't the back nine, is it?"

"I'm still shaking and sweating," Stephen replied. "I didn't know I had it in me."

"That's the point of the game," said Fergus. "But don't become complacent. The game gets more challenging, believe it or not. No matter what happens, keep playing. Let the demons appear, but don't let them distract you. This is one of the primary lessons of golf. Don't succumb to the demons."

They stood at the twelfth tee, facing a 500-yard stretch to the green. As Stephen looked out over the fairway, which sprawled out beneath the high perch of the elevated tee, hazards seemed to be appearing, one after the other: a stream, a boulder, several uprooted trees.

Fergus went first with a huge, heavy driver that far outsized any club a normal golfer would find in his bag. Stephen wondered how Fergus could wield it, given its enormous heft.

"This is a special back-nine club," he explained. "I'll let you use it, if you want it. On the other hand, your agility and speed might help you more in the long run."

Fergus hit the ball with the bulbous head of the massive club, and it was as though he had set off an explosion. The ball burst into the air and shot off at a low angle with so much speed that Stephen couldn't tell where it went.

"This will rouse the locals," said Fergus, and Stephen knew he wasn't referring to the human inhabitants of the village next to the course.

Stephen then took his turn and hit with a small, knobby seven wood. "Why do you want to stir up trouble?" he asked.

"Your health requires that your demons become visible to you. You need to know what they look like, sir. Illness is nothing more or less than the unleashing of a spirit in disguise. Here, in golf, you can see who your adversary is. For God's sake, man, your very being depends upon it."

They walked in the general direction of the green; Stephen looked around him on all sides as Fergus bent forward like a hunter intent on catching a glimpse of his prey. Then all hell broke loose. Fissures appeared in the earth, oozing hot, glowing red lava. Stephen ran, but Fergus shouted to him to stay on course for the green. "Don't be distracted from the game," he yelled.

Small monkey-shaped beings emerged with the lava and somehow were able to walk lightly over the molten magma. They kept appearing, until hundreds of them swarmed over the fairway of the twelfth hole. Their long pink tongues shot out over a foot in length, searching for something to taste. Stephen decided he wasn't going to be a snack for these vile creatures, but he had to zigzag over the fairway between hazards to avoid the monkeys. Their squeaky, piercing shrieks hurt his ears and made his innards tremble.

"They won't hurt you," shouted Fergus. "They're vegetarian."

Behind the monkeys rose a herd of bovine beings Stephen had never seen before. They looked like manatees with short legs and wide hooves. They grunted obscenely as they waddled out from under the earth onto the golf course, providing a low-pitched harmonic background to the pinched high squeaks of the monkeys.

"They are not vegetarian," Fergus warned loudly.

Stephen was tempted to run off the course, but he knew he had to trust Fergus, who repeatedly told him to stay focused on his game and remain within bounds. He walked, as fast as he could walk without running. He was trying to see above and beyond the monkeys in front of him and thus failed to see a large stone on the ground in his path. He tripped and sprawled on the trembling earth as the stump-legged beasts rumbled past him like a herd of stampeding cattle. He caught sight of Fergus with his arms spread out over the herd and assumed that only Fergus's powers had saved him.

Miraculously Stephen and Fergus finally arrived, through the din of stampede and wild shrieking, at the twelfth green.

"Hole out," said Fergus, "and we'll have a respite."

Stephen struggled to concentrate with the noise near unbearable in every direction and the manatee-like creatures pacing and glaring. He made a long putt, and Fergus followed him with a wide-curving shot from the edge of the green. Once the balls disappeared in the hole, an unsettling quiet immediately came upon the entire course, and the beasts went back to their dens in midearth.

Fergus appeared with a pot and two mugs in his hands. "Tea and biscuits," he said in a casual, friendly way.

The two golfers sat on the soft grass on the side of the mound that marked the thirteenth tee, drinking their tea.

"What is it about tea and these islands?" he asked Fergus.

"Ah, it's the ambrosia of these climates," he explained. "It isn't a mere liquid or an entertainment. Nor is it a necessity. Tea has the power to restore a sense of civility no matter what sort of feral outbreak has taken place. 'Tis one of the few drinks that touches the soul. Spirits do so as well, of course, but in a different way."

They had just finished their tea when Stephen heard a sound that was by now familiar—the erupting of the earth. Once again unfamiliar creatures came up from their haunts beneath the surface of the earth, and once again Fergus and Stephen battled to stay focused on their game. And so it went for the next several holes.

When they finally arrived at the eighteenth tee, Stephen felt exhausted. Like Odysseus spread out on the beach of an unknown island, like Dr. Livingstone on the trail in undiscovered Africa, he felt buffeted by his adventure. He would've liked to have hailed a taxi, gone to the airport, and flown home, but somewhere inside him was the faith that his ordeal, this fulcrum game of golf, was the key to his life's problems. And for no good reason, he trusted Fergus and didn't want to abandon him now.

The two men stood on the tee and looked around suspiciously. But as far as they could see there was an even green calm. A leaf hardly moved on a tree, and the course invited a leisurely game.

"Is this the calm before the storm?" Stephen asked. His clothes were torn, his face dirtied and scraped. He had little energy left and wore a defeated look.

"The calm is the worst thing," said Fergus. "This is the eighteenth hole, the last of the back nine, the final temptation and the ultimate battle. You have come, Stephen, with three requests regarding your marriage, your health, and your work. These are major concerns. Major indeed. To deal with them, we have had to face the nastiest demons, and now the deadliest calm."

"What do I do?"

"Keep your mind on the game. Focus on it to the end, when you hear the ball drop into the cup. It isn't over until the game is over."

"After what we've been through, that doesn't sound too difficult."

"I know. I know."

Fergus stood at the tee and set his ball high. He stretched his long body and cocked his club. He had chosen a driver, of course, for this last, long hole. He pulled back his club and torqued his body for the swing.

But Stephen noticed that in the middle of the arc toward the ball, Fergus lifted his shoulder with a jerk. The ball popped up like a cork from a bottle of champagne. It went off to the right not more than 50 yards.

"You see the trickery at work," Fergus said. "It's almost invisible and hardly dire. But they ask a dear price for your soul and mine. My task now is to get back on track and hit well toward the green. Stephen, whatever you do, don't do what I've just done. Keep your mind on the game."

Stephen took over on the tee and set his ball with determination. He would take great care with his swing. He decided to be safe and play a three wood—less chance of a wandering ball. He took three practice swings, each one smoother than the last. He was aware of a tendency to overpower the ball from his anxiety. He felt fully aware of what he was doing.

But just as the club came back behind his head, he glimpsed a familiar figure 100 yards out walking perpendicular to the fairway. It looked like Martin, from work. He put his club down and shaded his eyes with a hand.

"Martin?"

Fergus looked back at him sharply. "There's no one there, Stephen. Play your ball. Stay in the game."

"But I saw Martin. See, there he is. He's walking across our fairway. I'm delighted to see him."

Fergus rushed over and pushed Stephen to the tee. "Play the ball, Stephen. Your life is at stake. The game is everything. Don't be distracted."

Stephen broke free and hurried out into the fairway. He could see Martin walking slowly across the short grass toward the left rough. He felt a sudden ache of nostalgia and wished he could be home, finished with this game. Then he noticed the grim expression on Martin's face.

"What is it?'

"I'm glad I tracked you down. I've been going over the numbers—"

"And what?"

Martin shook his head sadly.

Stephen felt sick to his stomach. He wanted to weep, right there on the fairway. Then he heard Fergus shouting, "Go back to the game. It's an illusion."

Stephen tried to calculate all of this information in a second. Fergus was across from him on the other side of the fairway, watching to see what would happen.

"You're not Martin," Stephen said quietly to the creature now approaching him slowly.

"I gave you every chance I could," the vision said.

"Play on," urged Fergus.

"I must know if this is Martin," said Stephen loudly.

"It's an illusion. Everything but the game is an illusion," said Fergus.

"But I don't want to live in a world of games," said Stephen reasonably.

"The real world is a world of games," answered Fergus. "Play. Hit your ball. Golf is the only reality here."

Stephen stared at the being that looked like Martin. He looked closely. Then he turned and walked back to the tee and hit his ball. It went straight and long and high. Fergus smiled.

Both Stephen and Fergus were less than halfway to the green. They hit their second shots and both landed just short of the green, neither in one of the deep traps that lined the green. But Stephen's ball was at the edge of a wide, steep bunker. As he was considering how to navigate the complicated approach, he noticed a bench under a tree near the green. He felt infinitely tired and assaulted and thought that nothing in the world would be better than a brief break, a short rest.

He headed for the bench, and Fergus saw him. "No," he said. "You can rest later. That's what the clubhouse is for. The nineteenth hole. For God's sake, man, it's almost over. Don't falter now. You've almost survived the back nine, what?"

Stephen continued to walk toward the bench, but as he walked an inner debate of cosmic proportions carried on. Should he rest, or was Fergus right? Could golf be so important? Was it a holy route toward the deep game of life? Should he finish the game at all costs? Or was golf a silly way that old men chase a tiny ball and try to get it into a hole? Is it frivolous? Should he take care of himself, rest when his body complained? Why would it be so important to complete the game?

He approached the bench and touched the warm wood slats of its seat. It felt infinitely inviting. But Fergus's words and tone reverberated in his head. He trusted Fergus. Instead of sitting down, he veered left and went up to the green to prepare for the final putt. Fergus putted first and hit a dandy from 30 curving, undulating feet. Then Stephen took aim and holed it from 40 feet, making a semicircular curve. Doubtful, he reached into the hole for his ball and was relieved to feel it in the cup. He retrieved the ball and showed it to Fergus, who smiled knowingly.

Stephen and Fergus were walking from the eighteenth green to the clubhouse when they passed four women who were just about to begin their game. "You look like you've done the back nine," one of them said in a friendly way. "We heard that someone had dared and so we waited until now to play. Is it safe?"

"Safe as a game of golf will ever be," Fergus answered, winking at the man who had been at the reception desk, who seemed to have overseen the entire game. Stephen just nodded his head. He wasn't ready for intercourse with the world yet.

When he got home, Stephen found new harmony in his marriage and his home, and he was given a raise and a promotion at work. When he went to his oncologist, during the second week back, the doctor examined his test results and said, "All right. You've been on a juice fast and have had acupuncture every day, is that it? Your cancer's completely gone. You're supremely and firmly normal. What's your secret?"

"Golf," Stephen answered. "I learned that golf is a therapeutic game."

"Ah, yes," said the doctor. "All that peace and tranquility."

Stephen nodded, but his head was full of images from the game of golf that changed his life, the one that taught him that life is a game and you should never be distracted from it.

CHAPTER 17

Married to Golf

Wendy and Fred played golf every Friday morning of their married life. People at the country club would watch them tee off and head out onto the course, all the while admiring their togetherness. "Not many married people get along so well" was a common observation, spoken with a veneer of envy. But if the watchers could have gone out onto the course with Wendy and Fred this one particular day, they would have noticed that while Fred was smiling, Wendy wore a constant frown.

"Smell that fresh air!" Fred said. "There isn't a place in the world I'd rather be." He stood up to the tee, smiled in the wind, and slowly and gracefully swung his driver until it reached around behind his back and his right toe pointed into the ground. A photograph of him at that moment would have made an effective advertisement for the game as a pastime for perfect families.

Wendy shoved her tee into the hard ground with an effort that seemed to give her pleasure. She stood still at the ball, ready to take her hit, when Fred interrupted, "Uh, Wendy, your derriere should stick out just a little more." Wendy swung the club with a ferocity that Fred failed to notice, and the ball shot like a cannon from a naval vessel. They stuffed their drivers into their bags and walked out onto the fairway in search of their balls. Fred was whistling. Wendy was mumbling incoherently.

Each had driven about the same distance and their balls were about 15 yards apart halfway to the green. Fred was back a tad farther and so took the first iron shot. Again he swung slowly and harmoniously, lofting the ball high into the air and dropping it softly onto the edge of the green. Wendy grabbed her six iron and aimed practice chops at the poor ball before delivering a merciless hack that sent the white sphere sailing far beyond the green into a thick woodlot. She was not pleased.

"A little less pace," Fred shouted to her.

She made a postshot practice swing that dug up enough earth, with the ferocity of the stroke and the acute nature of the angle, to qualify as a minor excavation. Then she took a penalty and shot onto the green from the edge of the woods. Fred putted out, and Wendy three-putted.

On the next tee, Fred ventured a remark: "You look a little rattled today. Something wrong?"

"Do I look rattled?" Wendy asked.

"You're not yourself."

"I am myself, Fred. I'm always rattled. You are always calm, excessively calm, maddeningly calm."

"Wendy, how long have we been playing golf together?"

"An eternity."

"I was going to say nine years. We've enjoyed nine years of bliss on the golf course. People envy us. I think the equanimity of our game has kept our marriage together."

"I believe you're right," Wendy responded. "Golf has kept us together."

"Let's play the hole," said Fred. "It's a short one. Deceiving. It looks easy, but it isn't at all. Use your pitching wedge."

Wendy tightened her grip on the nine iron she had selected. She wondered if the shaft might fuse to her hand with the pressure she applied. "Fred, I don't tell you which club to use."

"That's because I'm a better golfer. I've played longer than you have."

"And?"

"And what?

"Say it—say it!"

"And I'm a man."

Wendy was a fan of murder mysteries. She often questioned what had attracted her to the genre, and now, as she wondered if she could implant her pitching wedge into Fred's skull so as to look like suicide, she had her epiphany. But what a shame to go to prison or death row simply for eliminating Fred from the scene. No, life would be richer than that. "Fred, don't be a misogynist," she said. "Plenty of women could beat you. In fact, I think I could."

Fred laughed. Possibly the biggest mistake of his life.

A week later, Fred and Wendy paraded, as usual, through the country club and headed for the links. This time, though, onlookers thought they saw a wrinkle in the marital bliss they appreciated so much and in which they found comfort. Fred didn't have the Astaire spring in his step and Wendy appeared less fused to Fred; in fact, she was walking several paces ahead of him. She took the lead as they rolled their pull carts out to the first tee. People gathered at the windows of the clubhouse to watch.

"I'm going to use a different strategy today," Wendy told Fred, as she stretched a club behind her back and then bent one leg and pulled out the other. "I'm going to start with my three wood and position the ball better for the green."

"Where did you learn that?" asked Fred with a frown.

"I saw it on television, and my golf instructor pointed it out to me as well."

"What golf instructor?"

"The one I hired at the end of our game last week."

"But we can't afford golf lessons for you."

"If you can play with your cronies twice a week without me, I can take one lesson a week, maybe even three."

Wendy swung her three wood with confidence and the ball went out to the knuckle of the dogleg just where she wanted it. Fred, a bit unnerved, sliced his drive away from the green and into the rough. Wendy hit the green on her next shot with a high loft, while Fred shanked one over into the rough opposite. Wendy waited for him on the green, studying her new notes on the course, while Fred tacked and hacked his way toward the green.

"I'm here in two," Wendy said, looking up from her notebook. "How are you doing?"

"I'd rather not say," said Fred. "I'll catch up. We have seventeen holes to go."

Wendy shrugged and dropped her 15-foot putt. Fred forgot to whistle as he finished the hole, and they strolled off the green.

By the fourth tee, a small crowd was tagging along behind the couple, eager to watch this war of the roses, knowing in a subliminal fashion that more was at stake here than a game of golf. Or maybe the game of golf was what was really at stake, and lives depended on its outcome. Tears and white knuckles were to be seen amid the onlookers. The drama of the occasion was lost on no one.

After the eighth green, Fred beckoned Wendy to join him on a bench for some quiet conversation.

"Do you remember?" he asked. "This is the very spot where I proposed to you and you surrendered your life to me."

"No," said Wendy. "This is where we decided to get married. I don't have any memory of surrender."

"A moment of humor," Fred offered. "Oh, please, let's end this game now and go to dinner at the clubhouse. We never did celebrate our engagement."

"But Fred," said Wendy, and at this the crowd drew closer, "I'd rather finish our game and celebrate our life together. An interrupted game is not a good metaphor."

"What I'm trying to say," Fred said with forced calm and honesty that almost touched his wife, "is that I'm embarrassed at my play, and the whole world seems to be watching. I'd like you to spare me."

"You are indeed a sensitive man, after all," said Wendy. "But I'm sure that completing this game will be the best thing for you and for me." At that, she got up and prepared for the ninth tee.

As the game progressed, Wendy's confidence soared and with that her game improved dramatically. Fred's got worse. After a particularly wayward drive on the eleventh tee, he asked Wendy if she would consider playing badly for a few holes just to let him catch up.

"Fred, the game is revealing your corrupt heart. You can't hide in a game of golf. Your tendency to cheat, brag, strut, or sink in self-pity becomes overwhelming.

I don't mean just you, but anyone who plays the game with their neuroses in play. This is your chance to heal yourself and shine. You have until the last putt to recover. All it takes is one stroke."

Fred had no idea what Wendy was talking about. But he knew that he had never sunk so low as to ask a golf partner to fake it, or take a dive, so to speak.

On the twelfth tee, Fred sat on the ground, sulking. "I can never walk off this course," he said to Wendy. "I couldn't withstand the embarrassment. I'll have to live here or kill myself. I'm telling you, Wendy, I have no choice."

The onlookers had dwindled to about three weepy people by now. Most felt they were eavesdropping on something much too personal for public viewing.

"That's all right with me," Wendy said. "I'm going to complete this game even if you hang yourself in a tree. Now, I'm going to be daring and try a seven wood on this hole."

The twelfth was a par three and the seven wood turned out to be a good choice. The ball landed two feet from the hole, and Fred, watching it make its arc with perfection, fell even deeper into despair. He slammed at his ball, which sputtered along the ground, bouncing in every direction, until it ended up in water. "The story of my life," he shouted to the sky.

On the fifteenth, Wendy and Fred both landed in a sand trap 50 yards from the green. Standing in the late afternoon sunshine in the broad, perfectly kept hazard, they both noticed that at some level the metaphors of the game were controlling their lives. Here they were, caught in a moment of decision, both in deep sand, stuck in a mire that kept them from their desired goal, and wondering if they had what it would take to get back to that most generous and expansive green.

"What club do you think I should use?" Fred asked.

Wendy was startled by the question. Then, taking in the magnitude of his query, she said calmly, "I'm going to use my seven iron."

"Rather unconventional," Fred said.

"I know," she said. "Why don't you try it as well?"

Fred walked back to his bag and replaced his sand wedge with a seven iron. He swung lightly at the ball and it sailed the 50 yards to the green and rolled toward the hole. Fred didn't whistle, but he smiled.

Wendy lofted her seven iron, too, and rolled her ball toward the hole, even with Fred's.

When they finished the game, first Wendy and then Fred tore up their scorecards and walked to the clubhouse. As they entered the lounge, dozens of people stood up and applauded. A four-piece jazz combo was playing that evening; and after they had dined well, Fred invited Wendy on to the dance floor. He did a few of his Fred Astaire turns and Wendy smiled and dipped and pretended she was Ginger Rogers.

CHAPTER 18

The Zen of Golf

James Crowe had what a psychoanalyst might call an idée fixe. He was consumed with the question of God's existence. His friends were tired of his long monologues about the history of the question and its existential relevance to him and his society. He had lost more than one girlfriend on that account. In another man's mind, the endless questioning could be exciting, even entertaining, but in James's case it was a bore.

James was raised a Catholic, and he interviewed perhaps a hundred priests to see if they could shed any light on his question. Every one of them came up short, even though it was their business, indeed their duty, to offer some substantive thought or idea.

Father Terry O'Shea told James to read Thomas Aquinas, the medieval theologian who offered five proofs for God's existence. James found the proofs too rationalistic to be convincing or intellectually comforting, except for the proof relating to beauty. James held the thought for a few minutes that the beauty of and in the world makes sense only if there is an artist of some description behind it all. Not in some naïve anthropomorphic sense, but at least an indication that there is more to life than what the scientists can measure and control. Father O'Shea eventually took to telling his secretary to inform James, if ever he should call, that the priest was out on a mission of mercy.

If you look closely, you can almost see a fixation manifesting itself in a person's body. They can't hide it and you can't avoid it. There's a synapse that has failed to ignite, a gap in a fine-toothed gear that normally keeps a person even and stable. It's unsettling and, indeed, James unsettled the average person who spent more than an hour with him. In the first 45 minutes or so of conversation you may think that you're talking to an interesting person focused on an interesting question, but at the 50-minute mark you suddenly notice the frozen eyeballs or the steep angle of the head and something bitter upsets your stomach and you begin to have thoughts about some other duty calling you.

James had a friend who was Buddhist. A teacher, maybe even a Zen master. James wasn't privy to the hierarchies of Buddhists, but he knew that his friend Toto was some sort of enlightened being.

"You must believe in God," James said to Toto one sunny afternoon when the teacher was sitting formally in an empty lot on James's block. "You couldn't give your life to meditation and serving humanity and praying unless God was somewhere."

"Buddhists don't believe in God," Toto said calmly. "We believe that belief in God chases away any proximity to God we could possibly enjoy."

"But that's why I like talking to you," said James said and he sat on the ground beside Toto. "Somehow your disavowal of God makes God vivid and present. You don't believe in him, and therefore he exists."

"You're going too far for me. We Buddhists don't play games like that. We don't say there is no God so we can feel good living with God. Let me tell you a story. There was once a monk who sought enlightenment with fervor that his master thought would destroy him. One day he began climbing a tall straight tree. He went up and up. He had gone higher than all the rooftops in his village when he suddenly looked down. There was no tree beneath him, only the one above him that he was climbing. At that moment he was enlightened and continued to climb. But the clarity in his mind lasted only a minute. He looked down again and feared for the tree that wasn't there. You know what happened."

"He fell."

"Like Adam. Very much like Adam. Exactly like Adam."

"But why don't you speak of God at all?"

"I can't and still be a religious person. In the best of worlds, 'God' is a pointing word. You sit and think about who or what God is, and then you go out into life and sense God in anything and everything. God is not the object of your thoughts and devotion, but the invisible thing, the nothingness, you find at the heart of things. The word points you to a revelation."

James was now feeling quite jittery. His eyes protruded from the sheer neurotic intensity of his curiosity. "How can you tell me this when you don't use the name of God at all, not even to point? You just sit."

"Exactly so," said Toto. "But look. I have a friend who does use the name and may have an answer for you. He is not a priest or a monk. He doesn't meditate in the usual way, but he is more of a theologian than anyone I know."

"Where can I find him?" James said, his eyes settling back into their sockets.

Toto looked undecided about answering the question. "I have a feeling you won't trust him at first."

"But he sounds perfect."

Tentatively Toto said, "You'll find him at the city golf course. He's the pro there."

James slumped forward and put his head in his hands. "Why can't I get a straight answer to my simple question? Now I have to go to Mr. Golf in the Kingdom. He'll drown me in metaphors and metaphysical crap. I'm not dumb, Toto. I'm serious. I'm already five miles in front of the theologian golf pro."

"You are five miles in front of yourself, my friend," Toto answered. "I don't have to tell you about Zen and the art of archery or flower arranging or the tea ceremony. It's a short step from there to golf."

James was now standing in front of the squatting monk, flailing his arms as he argued. "But don't you tell your students when you play golf, play golf, don't discuss philosophy?"

"You're trying to outwit me, James. You're defeating yourself."

"You really think I should go through the charade of making golf a spiritual exercise? I detest the game. It's pointless, aristocratic, capitalistic, and boring."

A week later James was at the city golf course looking for Sammy Weintraub. He asked around and was directed to a little man with a sizeable paunch, wearing a back-turned baseball cap.

"Hiya," the small man said when James approached him. "You here for a lesson?"

"Toto sent me," James said solemnly, hoping that mention of Toto's name would deliver him from the role of one seeking lessons in golf.

"Good. A real cool cat, Toto. So let's get started. Where are your clubs?"

James rocked on his feet, uncomfortable with the situation. "I'm interested in the ultimate game. You know, golf as a metaphor."

"You sure Toto sent you?" Sammy said.

"Toto. Buddhist. Monk. Master."

"Well, I teach golf. I don't care what religion you are. You want to learn, get a set of clubs. They rent them in the clubhouse. Meet me on the first tee."

James wondered if Sammy was either so sophisticated that he hid his status as a theologian, or if Sammy's theology was entirely in Toto's mind.

James rented some clubs and went to the first tee. Sammy put out a cigarette and pulled a driver from his bag. He coughed seriously for a moment and then placed a ball in position. He closed his eyes, opened them, and swung at the ball with perfect grace. James was stunned. He watched the ball shoot out from the tee at a medium angle and then rise into the air, straight and high. The "proof from beauty" entered his mind.

"Okay," Sammy said with a gravelly voice. "Try it."

James stood in front of the ball. He had played golf in high school. He wanted to do his best, and tried to remember all the instructions on how to hit a ball properly. He swung back, and Sammy coughed loudly.

"Nah," he said. "You got to be here and not be here. All at the same time. You're thinking. I can see all your thoughts trickling down your head. No thinking allowed. No trying. No nothing. Got it?"

James stood up to the ball once again. He cleared his mind. He tried to relax. He wanted to remember to keep his eye on the ball. He had heard that was rule number one. He was about to swing when Sammy coughed again.

"You are undoubtedly the worst student I ever had. You sure you want to play golf?"

"I'm more sure now than when I came here," James said, feeling his neck grow warm with rage.

"All right," Sammy said. "I won't look. You hit the ball any way you like. We take up the lesson on the second shot."

James blasted a ball far off to the right. The two grabbed their bags and walked down the fairway. James's ball was in the thick rough.

He was walking toward his ball, chiding himself for playing like a jerk, and deciding which club to use for his second shot, when Sammy yelled to him.

"Come here," he said. He led James to the top of a knoll that looked out over a small swamp full of cattails and a beaver dam and wild yellow irises. "Did you ever see anything so beautiful? And you were going to walk right past it. You might as well be playing miniature golf on green rugs and cement."

"But I thought I was supposed to concentrate on my game."

"Not on your game. On the game, the whole of it. The beauty of the course is part of the game. For some people, it's the major part. Where did you go to school, anyway?"

"I'm interested in God," said James.

"And you walk past this vision of natural beauty? I don't get it. People obsessed with God don't see anything but their ideas. No wonder they're always looking for God and waiting for him to come. Stupid, if you ask me. Are you a fanatic or something?"

James cleared his throat. "I'm a serious student of theology, and, to tell the truth, I don't know what I'm doing here."

"Well, la-dee-da," chanted Sammy. "I'm a serious student of the game of golf, the whole game of golf, and I say that if you can't play the game—what's that word you like to use? Holistically—you can forget about your theology."

"What I don't understand," James confessed, "is why Toto would send me here. I thought there might at least be a little cosmic consciousness, some inspiring metaphors."

"If you want a teacher who's into the deep meaning of golf, go find someone with bubbles of happiness floating out of his mouth. I'm a grunt-and-sweat kind of guy."

James looked glum. "You're right. I should get home now. This will just be a waste of your time and mine."

"Okay," said Sammy. "The best way to the parking lot is just past the first green. But we may as well finish the hole."

James walked over to his ball, which was lying behind a large rock. He looked at the green 150 yards away, and then at the impossible lie of the ball. He was staring at the ball when Sammy came over to him.

"This is not a metaphor," Sammy said. "This is you. Behind a rock. A real obstacle to getting ahead and onto the green. Stay in the game now. Don't waltz off into some metaphorical comet of inspirational enlightenment passing by. Your task is to get on the green in spite of the rock. There is no metaphor involved. Got that? Nothing matters now more than getting your ball closer to the green. Don't think about what it means. You just have to get to the green. Don't let your mind wander. Remember, the greatest temptation is the one about self-improvement. This game has nothing to do with self."

"But the game is stupid—it's a stupid game," James sputtered.

"Agreed. It's a stupid game. But that's irrelevant. Somewhere along the line you decided to play it. So don't quit."

James's attention shifted to the matter at hand. "I don't see how I can hit the ball without ricocheting it off the rock."

Sammy got down on his knees to look closely at the ball.

"Did you ever see a pro stand in a pond and hit his ball out of the water? Pros are superhuman. They know that the game asks things of them that are outrageous and impossible, and they don't back out. They use their imagination. They do the impossible. Now imagine how you could hit this ball and not catch the rock."

"I could move the rock."

"Not allowed."

"I could hit hard and take a lot of earth, straight up."

"Better yet, you could hit it softly with an ellipse in your swing vertical to the rock."

James stood at the ball and had an image of Sammy swinging his tee shot. Before he had a chance to think, his arms went up and then down through the ball. It sailed quite high and landed on the edge of the green. For the first time, Sammy smiled.

"Now, that's golf," he said, happy and complimentary.

Sammy then hit his second shot with that velvet swing of his and put his ball on the green nearer to the hole. Then the two men prepared for their putts.

"Okay," said Sammy, taking his putter from his bag as though it were adorned with precious stones. "This is the magic of golf. Putting. Either you sink these putts or you consider giving up the game. Everything is at stake, and it isn't as much about skill as magical thinking. A good putt is a thing of eternity, not time. Don't think of the ball traveling. Just pop it in the hole. Be in the hole receiving it in the cup of your hands. That's why I refer to the hole as a cup."

James said, "What if I miss?"

"You can't miss," said Sammy. "Don't think about it. Just put the ball in. Hole it."

"Of course, I might miss."

"You think you're a sinner, don't you, James?"

"Yes, I am a sinner. That's why I need God."

"You're not a sinner, James. You're a saint. If you know that, you'll be in the presence of God and that presence will be so devastating to all your neurotic worries that you'll stop waiting for him and wondering what he looks like. Now, putt like a saint."

James stepped up to the ball quickly, took a practice swing, and struck. Immediately he heard the ball careening inside the hole 30 feet away. Sammy holed his putt in a split second, as well. At that moment James could have sworn he saw a halo around Sammy's head.

They played 18 holes, each one more mysteriously otherwordly than the previous one. Sammy demonstrated his love of the game, and James saw how his celestial ability at the game came from his love rather than from his knowledge.

As they walked off the eighteenth green, James said, "Sammy, you are a theologian. I've just had a peak experience. I don't understand it."

"Nah," said Sammy. "I love the game and I love the course. Just let me play and I'm in bliss. No meanings. No theology. No self-improvement. Just the game."

Later in the week James stopped at the empty lot on his block, where Toto had just finished his sitting practice.

"How are you doing, my friend?" Toto asked.

"I've never been better. I seem to have more time on my hands and I'm sleeping well."

Toto was delighted. "And how was golf with Sammy?"

"Terrific. I'm going to play again with him later this week."

"And how about your quest?"

"What do you mean?"

"You've learned to love golf, haven't you?"

"I guess so. I want to play all the time now."

"And what about our previous conversation?"

"I don't think I remember it now," James said, scratching his head.

Toto reached into a bag and took out a small soapstone Buddha and placed it in James's hand. "I've wanted to give you this for a long time. I call him the Buddha of golf. He never stops playing, and he never uses a club. Pretty good golfer, huh?"

ABOUT THE AUTHOR

Best-selling author and psychotherapist **Thomas Moore** has written numerous books on spirituality, including *Writing in the Sand, Soul Mates, A Life at Work,* and the *New York Times* bestseller *Care of the Soul.* Born in Detroit, Michigan, Moore has devoted his life to the study of theology, world religions, Jungian and archetypal psychology, the history of art, and world mythology. He currently lives in New Hampshire.

Notes

Notes

Notes

NOTES

Notes

NOTES

Notes

NOTES

Notes

Hay House Titles of Related Interest

THE SHIFT, the movie,
starring Dr. Wayne W. Dyer
(available as a 1-DVD program and
an expanded 2-DVD set)
Watch the trailer at: **www.DyerMovie.com**

YOU CAN HEAL YOUR LIFE, the movie,
starring Louise L. Hay & Friends
(available as a 1-DVD program and
an expanded 2-DVD set)
Watch the trailer at: **www.LouiseHayMovie.com**

◇◇◇

LINDEN'S LAST LIFE: The Point of No Return Is Just the Beginning,
by Alan Cohen

THE NAPKIN, THE MELON, & THE MONKEY: How to Be Happy and Successful by Simply Changing Your Mind,
by Barbara Burke

THE SAINT, THE SURFER, AND THE CEO: A Remarkable Story About Living Your Heart's Desires,
by Robin Sharma

SARA, BOOK 3: A Talking Owl is Worth a Thousand Words,
by Esther and Jerry Hicks

SOLOMON'S ANGELS: Ancient Secrets of Love, Manifestation, Power, Wisdom, and Self-Confidence,
by Doreen Virtue

All of the above are available at your local bookstore, or may be ordered by contacting Hay House.

◇◇◇

We hope you enjoyed this Hay House book. If you'd like to receive our online catalog featuring additional information on Hay House books and products, or if you'd like to find out more about the Hay Foundation, please contact:

Hay House, Inc., P.O. Box 5100,
Carlsbad, CA 92018–5100

(760) 431-7695 or **(800) 654-5126**
(760) 431-6948 (fax) or **(800) 650-5115 (fax)**
www.hayhouse.com® • www.hayfoundation.org

◇◇◇

Published and distributed in Australia by:
Hay House Australia Pty. Ltd., 18/36 Ralph St.,
Alexandria NSW 2015 • *Phone:* 612-9669-4299
Fax: 612-9669-4144 • www.hayhouse.com.au

Published and distributed in the United Kingdom by:
Hay House UK, Ltd., 292B Kensal Rd., London W10 5BE
Phone: 44-20-8962-1230 • *Fax:* 44-20-8962-1239
www.hayhouse.co.uk

Published and distributed in the Republic of South Africa by:
Hay House SA (Pty), Ltd., P.O. Box 990, Witkoppen 2068
Phone/Fax: 27-11-467-8904 • www.hayhouse.co.za

Published in India by: Hay House Publishers India,
Muskaan Complex, Plot No. 3, B-2, Vasant Kunj, New Delhi 110 070
Phone: 91-11-4176-1620 • *Fax:* 91-11-4176-1630
www.hayhouse.co.in

Distributed in Canada by: Raincoast,
9050 Shaughnessy St., Vancouver, B.C. V6P 6E5
Phone: (604) 323-7100 • *Fax:* (604) 323-2600
www.raincoast.com

◇◇◇

Take Your Soul on a Vacation

Visit **www.HealYourLife.com®** to regroup, recharge, and reconnect with your own magnificence. Featuring blogs, mind-body-spirit news, and life-changing wisdom from Louise Hay and friends.

Visit **www.HealYourLife.com** today!

Mind Your Body, Mend Your Spirit

Hay House is the ultimate resource for inspirational and health-conscious books, audio programs, movies, events, e-newsletters, member communities, and much more.

Visit **www.hayhouse.com**® today and nourish your soul.

UPLIFTING EVENTS

Join your favorite authors at live events in a city near you or log on to **www.hayhouse.com** to visit with Hay House authors online during live, interactive Web events.

INSPIRATIONAL RADIO

Daily inspiration while you're at work or at home. Enjoy radio programs featuring your favorite authors, streaming live on the Internet 24/7 at **HayHouseRadio.com**®. Tune in and tune up your spirit!

VIP STATUS

Join the Hay House VIP membership program today and enjoy exclusive discounts on books, CDs, calendars, card decks, and more. You'll also receive 10% off all event reservations (excluding cruises). Visit **www.hayhouse.com/wisdom** to join the Hay House Wisdom Community™.

Visit **www.hayhouse.com** and enter priority code 2723 during checkout for special savings!

(One coupon per customer.)

Heal Your Life One Thought at a Time . . . on Louise's All-New Website!

"Life is bringing me everything I need and more."

— Louise Hay

Come to HEALYOURLIFE.COM today and meet the world's best-selling self-help authors; the most popular leading intuitive, health, and success experts; up-and-coming inspirational writers; and new like-minded friends who will share their insights, experiences, personal stories, and wisdom so you can heal your life and the world around you . . . one thought at a time.

Here are just some of the things you'll get at HealYourLife.com:

- DAILY AFFIRMATIONS
- CAPTIVATING VIDEO CLIPS
- EXCLUSIVE BOOK REVIEWS
- AUTHOR BLOGS
- LIVE TWITTER AND FACEBOOK FEEDS
- BEHIND-THE-SCENES SCOOPS
- LIVE STREAMING RADIO
- "MY LIFE" COMMUNITY OF FRIENDS

PLUS:
FREE Monthly Contests and Polls
FREE BONUS gifts, discounts, and newsletters

Make It Your Home Page Today!

www.HealYourLife.com®

HEAL YOUR LIFE®